MIDRASH
SINIM

MIDRASH
SINIM

HASIDIC LEGEND AND
COMMENTARY ON THE TORAH

YONG ZHAO

MIDRASH SINIM
HASIDIC LEGEND AND COMMENTARY ON THE TORAH

iUniverse books may be ordered through booksellers or by contacting:

iUniverse
1663 Liberty Drive
Bloomington, IN 47403
www.iuniverse.com
1-800-Authors (1-800-288-4677)

ISBN: 978-1-4917-7123-5 (sc)
ISBN: 978-1-4917-7121-1 (hc)
ISBN: 978-1-4917-7122-8 (e)

Print information available on the last page.

iUniverse rev. date: 07/22/2015

CONTENTS

FOREWORD

I will open my mouth with a parable;
I will utter dark sayings concerning days of old;
That which we have heard and known, and our fathers
have told us,
We will not hide from their children, telling to the
generation to come the praises of the LORD, and His
strength, and His wondrous works that He hath done.
—PSALM 78:2–4

The Torah was divinely revealed and relates to all of life. It contains eternal, perfect truth and hidden meanings that required elucidation. "Every letter and every word of the Torah contain numerous secrets" (Isaac Bashevis Singe: *In My Father's Court*). Throughout centuries, there has been enormous exegesis done and commentaries written on the Scriptures and its narratives. However, questions abound, and the controversy is fierce. For example:

- Why two different Creation narratives in the book of Genesis?
- The LORD had respect unto Abel and to his offering, but unto Cain and to his offering, He had not respect. Why?
- It was Ham who saw the nakedness of his father Noah, why did Noah curse Canaan and his offspring instead of Ham?
- *"For thee have I seen righteous before me in this generations"* (Gen.7:1). What on earth was Noah's righteousness? What significant transformation had occurred after the flood?
- Why did the LORD seek to kill Moses on his way to Egypt? And why did the LORD leave him alone when Zipporah cut off the foreskin of her son?

The above puzzles are satisfactorily solved in this book. I employ the "interpreting Scripture with Scripture" approach, and explore the

Scripture in light of Jewish tradition, archaeology, history, linguistics, literature, sociology, mathematics, geology, etc. As a result, the Torah codes are unlocked, and hidden meanings are revealed and expounded, through which the profundity of the Torah and Jewish traditions shines with even greater brilliance.

I also write of Adam, Eve, Noah, and Moses: Adam's grand tour with G-d, specific details about the fall, the righteous deed of Noah and Shem, and G-d's wondrous work on Moses' way into Egypt. These tales feature a style of Kabbalah and Aggadah. Besides, these tales are full of quotations from the Torah and therefore present a structure of jigsaw. Most importantly, they conform to the Torah and enhance Jewish traditions.

Chapter1: *Genesis Codes* Every organism has simultaneously two forms—invisible form and visible form—"invisible form" means "unformed substance" or "unformed frame," which is nonphysical and has neither dimension nor shape; "visible form" refers to the flesh which occupies a physical space. This chapter expounds the creation process, revealing that G-d created these two forms in sequence. The literal repetition, contradiction and fragment of Genesis 1-2 narrative are explained away.

Chapter 2: *Numbers and Mathematics in the Torah* This chapter discusses and unveils the complexities of numerical mysteries, Such as: the relationship among 10, 613, 248 and 365; the symbols of the six angles of Magen David; Jacob's age when he got married, etc. Step by step, readers are led to the profound message hidden in Scriptures over centuries.

Chapter 3: *Scripture Commentary I* Verses that range from Genesis 1:1 to Genesis 5:3 are successively interpreted, and innovative commentaries are therefore presented. For example: there is a micro-Torah embedded within the Torah; G-d was keeping the Sabbath prior to creating the world; Adam had lived in the Garden of Eden for one hundred years.

Chapter 4: *One Hundred Years of Glory* This chapter relates Adam's gripping days in the Eden. For example: his grand tour with G-d; his assistance in G-d's creation. Full of quotations from Torah, this chapter features Jigsaw structure, Kabbalah and Aggadah style.

Chapter 5: *Paradise Lost* This chapter unfolds the gripping process of the fall, describing how the couple successively committed seven errors so that G-d punished and expelled them from the Garden.

Chapter 6: *Good, Evil and Sin* Scriptures were explored within a different perspective from what one usually reads, and it is revealed that the Tree of Life was actually an atonement tree. For the first time ever, Torah theology was discovered and expounded.

Chapter 7: *Scripture Commentary II* Verses that range from Genesis 1:1 to Psalm 147 are interpreted, and innovative commentaries are therefore presented. For example: both Shem and Amram were righteous and wholehearted, Shem composed Psalm 93, and Amram was one of the seven righteous who had induced Shekhinah to descend from the heaven.

Chapter 8: *For Thee Have I Seen Righteous Before Me* This chapter reproduces the gripping details of the flood: the wickedness of men, the tremendous change of the heaven and the earth, Noah's zeal for men and for all the living things of all flesh. It reveals that the impact of the flood was two-fold: destroying the first world and generating a new one, with the latter more significant and profound.

Chapter 9: *The Story of Judah, the Hero* The narrative framework of Genesis 37-50 presents two concurrent stories of growth and change, featuring both Joseph and Judah. Judah being understood as a positive figure, this chapter points out that the storyline about Joseph is more prominent and explicit, while the one concerning Judah is mainly implied.

Chapter 10: *Now Therefore Go, Moses!* Featuring Kabbalah and Aggadah style, this chapter reproduces Moses' gripping experience on his way into Egypt and G-d's wondrous work there, describes Moses' ten evasions and G-d's persuasion, encouragement, promise and warning.

Chapter 11: *From Eden to China* Ancient Chinese characters, one after another, speak silently volumes about Genesis. Their close link is unveiled, and the messages about Genesis hidden in ancient Chinese characters are expounded.

PREFACE

I have always held a sense of harmony towards nature, ever since I was a child. When I was an under-graduate student, I used to travel everywhere and enjoy the beautiful nature sceneries. Gradually, I became curious about nature. "Why is nature so beautiful?", "how can it be so perfect and beautiful?" I was puzzled. I recalled those words of Edgar Allen Poe: "There is nothing of beauty that does not have some strangeness about it".

During the summer night of 1989, I used to lie down on the lawn to keep cool. At that moment, the vast sky and numerous bright stars were clearly visible. The more I stared at them, the more they appeared marvelous: although there were so many celestial bodies with astronomical volume in the universe, there was in a perfect order; every celestial body (the Earth, the Moon, the Sun, etc.) had its own fixed orbital and regular period for moving. It occurred to me that the cosmos was also as magical as nature. "How can the cosmos fall into and keep in such a concordant state?", "what drives and governs these celestial bodies?" Again, I was puzzled.

As my major was chemistry, I had learned the second law of thermodynamics. It states that in the course of a spontaneous change, the entropy of an isolated system must increase. Since the cosmos is itself an isolated system, we can extend the law to any system within the cosmos by noting that for any spontaneous change, the total entropy of the cosmos must increase. I guessed that there must be a supernaturalism which controlled the whole cosmos and kept the total entropy steady. "It is said that many the West believe in G-d, so, what is G-d? Is G-d just the supernaturalism?" With these questions, I went to a Church and got a bible for myself for the first time.

The unfolding of scriptures gives light. I can still remember how I was excited when I read Job 38-41. My questions were answered: it was G-d who created and governed the heaven and the earth! Since then, my delight has been in the Torah, and on the scripture I meditate day and night.

The Torah is a lamp to my feet and a light for my path. The more I read it, the more my soul is satisfied as with marrow and fatness. This book is the research results of studying the Torah over the years, it reflects my insights into the Scripture. Because I am a Hasidic Jew, I name the subtitle "Hasidic Legend and Commentary on the Torah".

Comments, questions and suggestions are welcome. Contact: Professor Yong ZHAO, School of Environmental Science and Engineering, Tianjin University, Tianjin 300072, P. R. China. E-mail: yzhao@tju.edu.cn

ACKNOWLEDGMENTS

I would like to acknowledge the enlightening and teaching of my friend ולדמן אהרן, who is the unique Chinese Jew I've met. Many scholars have contributed to this book and I wish to express my appreciation for their aid: Rabbi Dr. Yakov Nagen (the Yeshiva of Otniel, Israel), Mr. Selomo (Mechon Mamre, Israel), Professor Shelley Fisher Fishkin (Stanford University, USA), Prof. Dr. Stefan Schreiner (Universität Tübingen, Germany), Professor Admiel kosman (Potsdam University, Germany), Professor Stephen Sadow (Northeastern University, USA), Professor Joel Rappel (Boston University, USA). Their comments, questions and suggestions have been carefully studied, found to be of substantial merit, and incorporated into the text wherever possible.

Torah quotations are taken from Jewish Publication Society 1917 Edition, and Yong Zhao thank very much Jewish Publication Society for the granting permission.

CHAPTER 1

Genesis Codes

1. Two Stages, three steps

Myths or history: is that the question?

In the book of Genesis, both chapter 1 and chapter 2 relate the Creation. However, there are obvious discrepancies between these two consecutive accounts on the aspects of content, structure, and style. How did the Torah come to be written? Who was/were the author? Opinions are divided, and controversies are fierce.

Critics allege that the Torah is a product of imagination and fancy. Graf-Wellhausen Documentary Hypothesis—the leading academic theory—states that, separate texts developed over centuries, multiple authors were responsible for producing them, and one or more redactors braided them together, leaving many literal flaws.

Advocators insist on the Mosaic authorship, defending the reliability and inerrancy of Scriptures. But they fail to satisfactorily explain the literal repetition, contradiction and fragment of the Torah narrative.

Myths or history: that is not the question.

In fact, the Torah is the LORD's revealed word to Moses, and it is true history record. As for the literal repetition, contradiction and fragment of the Torah narrative, I will explain them away, expound on how the two creation accounts precisely document and vividly demonstrate the LORD's work.

Scriptures (Psa. 139:15–16) implies that, everyone has simultaneously two forms—visible form and invisible form—"visible form" refers to the flesh which occupies a physical space; "invisible form" means "unformed substance" or "unformed frame," which is nonphysical and has neither dimension nor shape.

My frame was not hidden from Thee, when I was made in secret, and curiously wrought in the lowest parts of the earth. Thine eyes did

*see mine unformed substance, and in Thy book they were all written—
even the days that were fashioned, when as yet there was none of them*
(Psa. 139:15–16).

The *"unformed substance"* is invisible form, and can be written in
LORD's book. The flesh is visible form, and can be fashioned on the
earth. In light of these verses, everyone has simultaneously unformed
substance and flesh. Therefore, when the LORD created human beings,
He successively created their unformed substance and flesh, and this
process is recorded in sequence by Genesis 1 and Genesis 2.

① In Genesis 1, the unformed substance of human beings were
  created and wrote in the LORD's book *"And God created man
  in His own image, in the image of God created He him; male
  and female created He them"(Gen. 1:27).*

② In Genesis 2, their fleshes were fashioned in the Garden of Eden
  *"Then the LORD God formed man of the dust of the ground, and
  breathed into his nostrils the breath of life; and man became
  a living soul"(Gen. 2:7), "And the LORD God caused a deep
  sleep to fall upon the man, and he slept; and He took one of his
  ribs, and closed up the place with flesh instead thereof. And the
  rib, which the LORD God had taken from the man, made He a
  woman, and brought her unto the man"(Gen. 2:22-23)*

That is why the first two chapters of Genesis comprise two creation
accounts of human beings. The creation process is explained further as
below:

According to biologic taxonomy, plants, animals and human beings
are organisms, pertaining to living matters, while stars, the heaven and
the earth are in-organisms, pertaining to nonliving matters. Organisms
have simultaneously unformed substance and flesh, and their unformed
substance were created and written in the LORD's book (Genesis 1)
before their flesh were created (Genesis 2); In-organisms have only
visible form, and were created directly in one step—*For He spoke, and
it was; He commanded, and it stood* (Psa. 33:9)—as Genesis 1 records.

More specifically, the LORD created organisms in three steps:

- The process of creating human beings:

① Step 1: proclaiming the plan
   And the LORD said: "Let us make man in our image, after our likeness; and let them have dominion over the fish of the sea, and over the fowl of the air, and over the cattle, and over all the earth, and over every creeping thing that creepeth upon the earth." (Gen. 1:26)
   This verse indicates that the LORD first proclaimed the creation plan of human beings.

② Step 2: creating the unformed substance
   And G-d created man in his own image, in the image of G-d created he him; male and female created he them (Gen. 1:27).
   This verse indicates that after proclamation, the LORD then created and wrote the unformed fleshes of male and female in His book[1], and yet their flesh was not shaped.

③ Step 3: fashioning the flesh
   Then the LORD G-d formed man of the dust of the ground, and breathed into his nostrils the breath of life; and man became a living soul (Gen. 2:7).
   And the LORD G-d caused a deep sleep to fall upon the man, and he slept; and He took one of his ribs, and closed up the place with flesh instead thereof. And the rib, which the LORD G-d had taken from the man, made He a woman, and brought her unto the man (Gen. 2:21–22).
   These verses indicate that the LORD finally shaped the first man and the first woman in the Garden of Eden.

- The process of creating plants:

① Step 1: proclaiming the plan
   And G-d said: "Let the earth put forth grass, herb yielding seed, and fruit-tree bearing fruit after its kind, wherein is the seed thereof, upon the earth." And it was so (Gen. 1:11).

First, the LORD proclaimed the creation plan of plants.

② Step 2: creating the unformed substance

And the earth brought forth grass, herb yielding seed after its kind, and tree bearing fruit, wherein is the seed thereof, after its kind; and G-d saw that it was good (Gen. 1:12).

Then the LORD created and wrote the unformed substance of plants in His book according to the plan proclaimed.

③ Step 3: fashioning the flesh

And out of the ground made the LORD G-d to grow every tree that is pleasant to the sight, and good for food; the tree of life also in the midst of the garden, and the tree of the knowledge of good and evil (Gen. 2:9).

Finally, in the third step, the LORD created the plants in the Garden of Eden.

• The process of creating animals:

(1) The creation plan of fishes and birds

① *And G-d said: "Let the waters swarm with swarms of living creatures, and let fowl fly above the earth in the open firmament of heaven."* (Gen. 1:20)

First, the LORD proclaimed the creation plan of fishes and birds.

② *So G-d created the great creatures of the sea and every living and moving thing with which the water teems, according to their kinds, and every winged bird according to its kind. And G-d saw that it was good* (Gen. 1:21).

Then the LORD created the unformed substances of fishes and birds, wrote in His book.

4

(2) The creation plan of cattle, creeping things, and beasts

① *And G-d said: "Let the earth bring forth the living creature after its kind, cattle, and creeping thing, and beast of the earth after its kind." And it was so* (Gen. 1:24).

First, the LORD proclaimed the plan and design about the creation of cattle, creeping things, and beasts.

② *And G-d made the beast of the earth after its kind, and the cattle after their kind, and every thing that creepeth upon the ground after its kind; and G-d saw that it was good* (Gen. 1:25).

Then the LORD created the unformed substances of cattle, creeping things, and beasts, and wrote them in His book.

(3) Fashioning the flesh

And out of the ground the LORD G-d formed every beast of the field, and every fowl of the air; and brought them unto the man to see what he would call them; and whatsoever the man would call every living creature, that was to be the name thereof (Gen. 2:19).

At last, the LORD fashioned the animals in the Garden of Eden.

In comparison, the creation of organisms is similar to housing construction, which contains two fundamental stages:

Stage 1: planning and designing

The first thing is to complete a design scheme: the builder takes into consideration every aspect—from outlook to details of corridors, staircases, doors, and windows. Also he would produce an elaborated design, which is specific to millimeter scale, of the structure of these details. After completing the design, he makes a set of construction drawings as well.

Stage 2: Constructing

After having carried out rigorous investigation and research of the site and making preparations for the building materials, the builders build the house according to the construction drawings: first, he digs out a foundation deep to load-bearing soil, then, he constructs a steel frame. After that, he casts concrete to finish the basis of the building. This process of constructing a steel frame and then casting concrete will be repeated on each layer until finishing the construction.

Similarly, the LORD created organisms in two stages. The first stage contained two steps: step 1 is "proclaiming the creation plan", and step 2 is "producing the design drawing—designing and drawing the blueprint in His book, namely, creating and writing the unformed substance of lives in His book". The second stage contained step 3, "putting the blueprint into effect, namely, making the flesh of organisms".

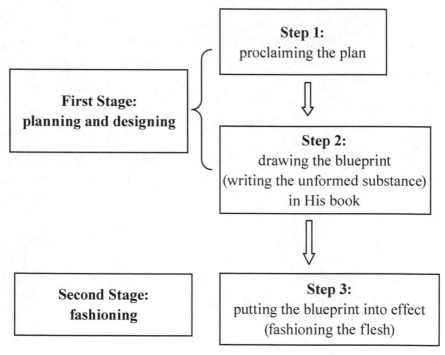

Illustration 1-1 Creation sequence of lives

In conclusion, the first two chapters of Genesis detail the creation process in sequence. Genesis 1 accounts for the first stage, describing the plan and the blueprints of creation. Genesis 2 records the second stage, introducing how the LORD put the blueprints into effect and made the lives on the earth.[2]

Table 1-1: The Creation Sequence

Stage 1 (Gen. 1:1–2:3)	1st day	Creating light (in-organism)	*"Let there be light." And there was light* (Gen. 1:3)
	2nd day	Creating the heaven (in-organism)	*And God made the firmament ... and it was so* (Gen. 1:7–8)
	3rd day	① Creating the earth (in-organism); ② Writing the unformed substances of plants in His book	① *"Let the dry land appear." And it was so* (Gen. 1:9) ② *"Let the earth put forth grass." And it was so. And the earth brought forth grass* (Gen. 1:11–12)
	4th day	Creating celestial bodies (in-organism)	*And God made the two great lights ... and the stars* (Gen. 1:14–16)
	5th day	Writing the unformed substances of fishes and birds in His book	*And God created the great sea-monsters, and every living creature that creepeth, wherewith the waters swarmed ... and every winged fowl after its kind* (Gen. 1:21)
	6th day	Writing the unformed substances of living creatures and men and women in His book	*"Let the earth bring forth the living creature after its kind ... And God said: "Let us make man in our image, after our likeness* (Gen. 1:24–27)
	7th day	Resting	*And on the seventh day God finished His work which He had made; and He rested on the seventh day from all His work which He had made* (Gen. 2:1–3)

Stage 2 (Gen. 2:4–2:22)	Later time	Fashioning Adam	*Then the LORD God formed man of the dust of the ground* (Gen. 2:7)
		Creating plants	*And out of the ground made the LORD God to grow every tree that is pleasant to the sight* (Gen. 2:9)
		Fashioning animals	*And out of the ground the LORD God formed every beast of the field, and every fowl of the air* (Gen. 2:19).
		Fashioning Eve	*And the rib, which the LORD God had taken from the man, made He a woman* (Gen. 2:22).

2. Classic Questions and Explanations

(1) When were the angels created?

Jochanan said it was on the second day, because it is written, *Who layeth the beams of his chambers in the waters; Who maketh the clouds his chariot; Who walketh upon the wings of the wind.* (Psa. 104:3) Channina put that it was on the fifth day because the Torah states, *Above him stood the seraphim: each one had six wings; with twain he covered his face, and with twain he covered his feet, and with twain he did fly* (Isa. 6:2).

Before the Fall, Adam walked with the LORD. At that time, no angels were needed. After the couple were driven out of the Garden of Eden, angels were created, who acted as the LORD's servants and messengers to exercise His decree and accomplish His mission.

(2) When were Adam and Eve created?

On which day was Adam created? And on which day was Eve created?

In Genesis 1, Adam's unformed substance was created on the sixth day. In Genesis 2, Adam's flesh was formed on the first day after the seventh day (i.e. Sabbath). Thus, it was Sunday.

When was Eve created? On Friday (to be detailed in chapter 5: Paradise Lost).

The sequence of the creation is shown as follows:

Table 1-2: Creation Sequence

1st day	light
2nd day	the heaven
3rd day	dry land, unformed substances of plants
4th day	celestial bodies
5th day	unformed substances of fishes and birds
6th day	unformed substances of organisms
7th day (Sabbath)	resting
8th day (Sunday)	Adam
Later time	plants, animals
100 years later (Friday)	Eve

(3) The heavens and the earth: which was created first?

The school of Shammai says first the heavens were created and then the earth; as it is written, *In the beginning G-d created the heaven and the earth* (Gen. 1:1). The school of Hillel says first the earth was created and then the heavens; as it is written, *In the day that G-d made earth and heaven* (Gen. 2:4).

Said the sages of Hillel to the sages of Shammai, "According to your interpretation, would one build a loft before one builds the house? For it is written, *It is he that buildeth his chambers in the heavens, and hath founded his vault upon the earth*" (Amos 9:6). Said the sages of Shammai to the sages of Hillel, "According to your interpretation, would one make the footstool and then make the chair? For it is written, *Thus saith Jehovah, Heaven is my throne, and the earth is my footstool*" (Isa. 66:1)[3]

The truth is like this:

In the first stage of creation, light and the heaven were created prior to dry land (the earth). So the Torah states, *In the beginning G-d created the heaven and the earth* (Gen. 1:1). But in the second stage of creation, there is a different situation:

① After Adam was created and became a living soul, the LORD named all the celestial bodies.

   In the Torah, name is essential and significant. It determines the essence and nature, even the existence of a thing itself. Without name, nothing could be a real and complete being. Although the celestial bodies were created in the first stage, they were not named, so they were not complete and real beings yet. Only after Adam was created and became a living soul, were celestial bodies named. That is to say, Adam became a living soul before the celestial bodies became complete and real existences. Adam pertained to the earth while the celestial bodies to the heaven.

② First Adam's flesh was made, and then his soul and life were given. Adam's flesh pertained to the earth, while his soul and life pertained to the heaven.

③ The creation of Adam was previous to that of the angels. Adam pertained to the earth, while the angels to the heaven.

Therefore, the Torah states, *These are the generations of the heaven and of the earth when they were created, in the day that the LORD G-d made earth and heaven* (Gen. 2:4).

CHAPTER 2

Numbers and Mathematics of the Torah

1. Number 1, 6, and 7

6 is the number pertaining to humans, 1 and 7 are the numbers pertaining to the LORD.

It was on the sixth day of creation that the plan and design of creating men was made, and men's fates were destined. Jacob had twelve sons; Israel was divided into twelve tribes, and one solar year consists of twelve months. Twelve is a multiple of six.

7 is the number pertaining to the LORD, because the seventh day is the holy Sabbath. Also, 1 is the number pertaining to the LORD, because it means uniqueness, indicating that the LORD is unique and singular in the world. 1 is inseparable, and the LORD is inseparable.

2. Number 10, 613, 248, and 365

There are 613 mitzvoth, 248 of which are active and 365 of which are passive.

Ten Commandments were exactly written with 613 letters (Exod. 20:1–14), demonstrating the close link between 10 and 613.

A number game demonstrates the relation among 10, 613, 248 and 365:

10=6+1+3, and **10**=(1+4)+(1+4)

(1) **10**=6+1+3

6, 1, and 3 can be combined together to form **613**, the total number of mitzvoth.

(2) **10**=(1+4)+(1+4)

1 and 4 can be combined together to form 14.

① The first 14 is the sum of 2, 4, and 8.

2, 4, and 8 can be combined together to form **248**, the number of active mitzvoth.

② The second 14 is the sum of 3, 6, and 5.

3, 6, and 5 can be combined together to form **365**, the number of passive mitzvoth.

The relation among these four numbers is illustrated as below:

$$5 = 1 + 4 \Rightarrow 14 = 2 + 4 + 8 \Rightarrow \underline{248}$$

$$\underline{10} = 5 + 5 = 6 + 1 + 3 \Longrightarrow 613$$

$$5 = 1 + 4 \Rightarrow 14 = 3 + 6 + 5 \Rightarrow \underline{365}$$

3. Twenty-two Hebrew Letters

In the beginning G-d created the heaven and the earth (Gen. 1:1).

1 is the number pertaining to the LORD, and 1 is also the foundation and source of all other numbers. It is 1 that the LORD used to create the world.

A similar number game is repeated:

1) 1 is the sum of 1 and 0;
   1 and 0 can be combined together to form 10.
2) 10 is the sum of 1 and 9;
   1 and 9 can be combined together to form 19.
3) 19 is the sum of 1, 4, 9, and 5;
   1, 4, 9, and 5 can be combined together to form 1495
4) 1495 is the sum of twenty two different numbers, from 1 to 400:
   1495=1+2+3+4+5+6+7+8+9+10+20+30+40+50+60+70+80+90
   +10+200+300+400

There are twenty-two Hebrew letters in all, each representing one specific number. See the table below.

Table 2-1: Letters and Numbers

Letter	Number	Letter	Number	Letter	Number	Letter	Number
Alef	1	*Zayin*	7	*Mem*	40	*Qof*	100
Bet	2	*Het*	8	*Nun*	50	*Resh*	200
Gimel	3	*Tet*	9	*Samek*	60	*Shin*	300
Dalet	4	*Yod*	10	*Ayin*	70	*Tav*	400
He	5	*Kaf*	20	*Pe*	80	-	-
Vav	6	*Lamed*	30	*Tsadi*	90	-	-

These twenty-two Hebrew letters exactly correspond to the twenty-two numbers that add up to 1495. Therefore, the heaven and the earth originated from the Hebrew letters.

4. Seven Pillars

Wisdom hath builded her house, she hath hewn out her seven pillars (Prov. 9:1).

The world could be compared to a house, and it has seven pillars: Genesis, Exodus, Leviticus, Numbers, Deuteronomy, Talmud, and Zohar.

The world has other seven pillars, namely seven righteous men who induced the divine glory to descend from heaven to the earth): Enoch, Noah, Abraham, Isaac, Jacob, Amram, and Moses (see Chapter 6:3 The Departure and Return of Shechinah, and Chapter 7:13 Amram: A Righteous and Wholehearted Man)

5. Six Angles of Magen David

Magen David is the symbol of Israel and Jewish people. It conveys profound meanings. The following is my interpretation on Magen David:

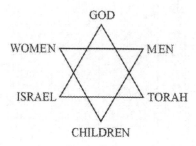

Fig 2-1: The meaning of Magen David

In a clockwise direction, the six angles symbolize the LORD, men, the Torah, children, Israel, and women. The Torah and Israel are two precious gifts from the LORD. So the LORD, the Torah, and the land of Israel form an elementary unit, the upside triangle. Men, women, and children constitute the family; hence they form another elementary unit, the downward triangle.

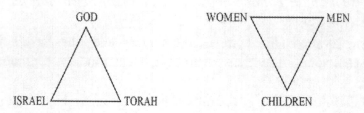

Fig 2-2 the upward triangle   **Fig 2-3 the downward triangle**

① The First Diagonal: the LORD *vs.* Children

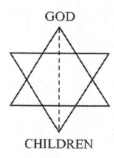

Fig. 2-4 The first diagonal

To have children is the first mitzvah. *Be fruitful, and multiply, and replenish the earth* (Gen. 1:28a).

14

Children are the blessing of the LORD. *Lo, children are a heritage of the LORD; the fruit of the womb is a reward* (Psa. 127:3).

The key to sustaining, strengthening, and expanding Jewish faith and tradition is children. Where there are children, there is hope. *And thou shalt teach them diligently unto thy children, and shalt talk of them when thou sittest in thy house, and when thou walkest by the way, and when thou liest down, and when thou risest up* (Deut. 6:7).

② The Second Diagonal: Men *vs.* Israel (the Promised Land)

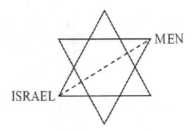

Fig. 2-5 The second diagonal

As mentioned earlier, the land of Israel was granted to Jews,

① *Command the children of Israel, and say unto them ... this shall be your land according to the borders thereof round about." (Num. 34:2–12).*

② *Thus saith the LORD G-d: "This shall be the border, whereby ye shall divide the land for inheritance according to the twelve tribes of Israel, Joseph receiving two portions ... So shall ye divide this land unto you according to the tribes of Israel." (Ezek. 47:13–21)*

This land of Israel is the holy, uniquely Jewish land at its very essence, remaining associated with Jewish people forever. The sacred mission of Jewish men is to conquer, inhabit, manage, and guard it. They should strive—sweat, bleed and even sacrifice—for the mission.

③ The Third Diagonal: Women *vs.* Torah

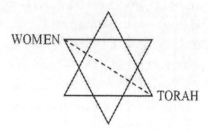

Fig. 2-6 The third diagonal

Women are the first teacher of human beings. Jewish tradition maintains that the Torah was primarily given to women.[4] Thus women and the Torah can form a diagonal.

6. One Drank, Another Ate (Gen. 18:7–8)

According to mitzvah, milk and meat should not be had simultaneously, *thou shalt not seethe a kid in its mother's milk* (Exod. 23:19). When Abraham simultaneously set curd, milk, and calf before the angels, how did they eat? Traditionally thinking, they ate one thing first, then, the other several hours later (three hours or six hours later). A reasonable explanation should be that these two angels had curd, milk, and calf simultaneously: one ate the calf, while another drank the milk and ate the curd.

7. The Age of Jacob When He Got Married

How old was Jacob when he got married? The deduction is as below:

Table 2-2: Deduction I

Scriptures	Deduction
And Jacob lived in the land of Egypt seventeen years: so the days of Jacob, the years of his life, were a hundred forty and seven years (Gen. 47:28).	Jacob reached Egypt at age 130 (147-17=130)

① *Joseph was thirty years old when he stood before Pharaoh king of Egypt. And Joseph went out from the presence of Pharaoh, and went throughout all the land of Egypt* (Gen. 41:46); ② *And the seven years of plenty, that was in the land of Egypt, came to an end* (Gen. 41:53); ③ *For these two years hath the famine been in the land: and there are yet five years, in which there shall be neither plowing nor harvest* (Gen. 45:6).	Joseph reunited with his brothers at age 39 (30+7+2=39).

1. When they met again, Jacob was 130 years old and Joseph was 39 years old. Therefore, Jacob was 91 years old when Joseph was born.

Table 2-3: Deduction II

Scriptures	Deduction
① *And it came to pass, when Rachel had borne Joseph, that Jacob said unto Laban: "Send me away, that I may go unto mine own place, and to my country. Give me my wives and my children for whom I have served thee, and let me go; for thou knowest my service wherewith I have served thee."*(Gen. 30:25–26) ② *These twenty years have I been in thy house: I served thee fourteen years for thy two daughters, and six years for thy flock; and thou hast changed my wages ten times* (Gen. 31:41).	Joseph was born in the selfsame year when Jacob left Laban. By that time, he had lived with Laban for twenty years.

2. Jacob left Laban at age 91. Until then, he had lived with Laban for twenty years. So he must have been 71 years old when he started to live with Laban. *And Jacob served seven years for Rachel; and they seemed unto him but a few days, for the love he had to he* (Gen. 29:20). It was after he had served Laban for seven years that Jacob got married. Because, so Jacob got married at age 78.

8. Circumcision on the Eighth Day (Gen. 17:13).

The first eight days of a newborn baby correspond to the first eight days of creation. Adam's flesh was shaped on the eighth day of creation. It was on that very day that the LORD marked his flesh and breathed into his nostrils the breath of life, and man became a living soul. Hence a boy needs to be circumcised on the eighth day of his birth, so that the LORD's covenant shall be in his flesh for an everlasting covenant.

9. Minyan: Ten (Gen. 18:32–33).

Though Sodom and Gomorrah were full of the wicked, the LORD would not destroy them as long as there were at least ten righteous men in each city; thus the lives of the wicked could have been spared. Where there are ten righteous men get together, there are the LORD's mercy and redemption.

10. Fourteen Tribes and Seventy Elders

And unto Moses He said: "Come up unto the LORD, thou, and Aaron, Nadab, and Abihu, and seventy of the elders of Israel; and worship ye afar off; and Moses alone shall come near unto the LORD; but they shall not come near; neither shall the people go up with him." (Exod. 24:1–2)

And the LORD said unto Moses: "Gather unto Me seventy men of the elders of Israel, whom thou knowest to be the elders of the people, and officers over them; and bring them unto the tent of meeting, that they may stand there with thee." (Num. 11:16)

In both cases, the number of summoned elders was 70. Why? How did Moses select these seventy elders?

The traditional explanation is as follows. The Israelites were divided into twelve tribes. Moses ordered each tribe to select six persons, and thus seventy-two candidates in total were selected. Then, he made seventy-two cards, with two cards marked differently. The candidates were asked to draw cards at random; those who chose the marked card would be weeded out, and there were seventy elders left. This explanation is untenable. If the number of summoned elders was a multiple of twelve—for instance—60 or 72, it would be much easier for Moses to choose. Why did the LORD not simply do so?

When the Israelites escaped from Egypt, large quantities of alien followed them. The aliens comprised alien nobles and alien slaves:

① *A mixed multitude* (Exod. 12:37–38) means the alien;

② *All the men of Israel, your little ones, your wives* (Deut. 29: 9) stands for the Israelites, while *thy stranger that is in the midst of thy camp, from the hewer of thy wood unto the drawer of thy water* (Deut. 29: 9) represents the alien nobles and slaves.

When they were in the wilderness, Moses was commanded to select elders from both the Israelites and the aliens. The alien nobles and slaves were taken as two additional tribes. So there were fourteen tribes altogether. Each tribe elected five elders, and there were seventy elders in total. It is exactly the number commanded by the LORD.

The aliens not only elected their representatives, but also brought offerings to the LORD.

And the LORD called unto Moses, and spoke unto him out of the tent of meeting, saying: "Speak unto the children of Israel, and say unto them: When any man of you bringeth an offering unto the LORD, ye shall bring your offering of the cattle, even of the herd or of the flock (Lev. 1:1–2).

It is said that there are some errors in English translation; the original Hebrew text is "Speak unto the children of Israel, and say unto them, when any man bringeth an offering unto the LORD". The original Hebrew text showed clearly that not only the Israelites but also the aliens sacrificed to the LORD.

When the Israelites escaped Egypt, the aliens followed; when the Israelites sent the elders to the LORD, they did the same; when the Israelites brought offerings to the LORD, they were with them; when the Israel entered the Promised Land, they also went there.

The LORD took both the Israelites and the aliens as his Chosen People. In the wilderness of Sinai, the Torah was given not only to the

Israelites but also to the aliens. In this sense, the Torah belongs to all nations.

Exodus was an epoch-making event, because it was the first time in history that on a large scale the aliens converted to Judaism.

CHAPTER 3

Scripture Commentary 1

1. Micro-Torah Embedded within the Torah

In the beginning G-d created the heaven and the earth (Gen. 1:1).

The Torah's first word, *bereishit*, is an acronym for *B reishit*—"two firsts" (in Hebrew, the second letter of the alphabet, *bet*, is also the number *two*). Why does the Torah begin with *bet* instead of the first one, *aleph*? Some Jewish sages hold that *bet* is the first letter of *berachah* (bless), while *aleph* is the first letter of *arriah* (curse), and that's why *alef* is skipped at the beginning of the Bible. Since *bet* is also the number *two*, some others believe that this is to say that the world was created for the sake of two things called "first" (*reishit*): the Torah (Prov. 8:22) and the people of Israel (Jer. 2:3); and Otiyot d'Rabbi Akiva held that it was because the LORD said, "I built two palaces--one above and one below. I formed the laws of nature, and I established the life of the world to come."

In fact, there is a micro-Torah, narrative frame of which is embedded within that of the Torah. The first verse, *In the beginning G-d created the heaven and the earth*, is not only the opening words of the Torah, but also that of a micro-Torah.

The micro-Torah comprises the first three chapters of Genesis. In other words, the stories of creation and the Garden of Eden make up the micro-Torah, which can be divided into five parts and correspond to the five volumes of the Torah. Illustration is as below and will be detailed in Chapter 7.

The first part (Gen. 1–2:3): The LORD created the in-organisms and created the unformed substances of organisms. This part corresponds to the first volume of the Torah, *Genesis*. In this volume, the LORD created the heaven and the earth, made man, and chose the Israelites.

The second part (Gen. 2:4–14): the LORD formed man from the dust of the ground and made him a living soul that could stand on the ground. This part corresponds to the Torah's second volume, ***Exodus***, in which the LORD delivered the Israelites out of the hand of the Egyptians and made them the Chosen People.

The third part (Gen. 2:15–17): The LORD informed Adam of what he may eat and what shall not, and taught him to live in the Garden of Eden. This part corresponds to the third volume of the Torah, ***Leviticus***, in which the LORD declared to the Israelites such statutes and ordinances as what they may eat and what shall not, and He taught them to live a holy life.

The fourth part (Gen. 2:8–3:21): This part records the deeds of Adam and Eve in the Garden of Eden, during which they sinned and were punished. It corresponds to the Torah's fourth volume, ***Numbers***. This volume records the deeds of the Israelites in the wilderness, during which they sinned and were punished.

The fifth part (Gen. 3:22–24): In this part, the LORD expelled Adam and Eve from the Garden of Eden. Before that, the LORD called unto them and reiterated the commandments, statutes, and ordinances that they were taught to keep and do. This part corresponds to the Torah's fifth volume, ***Deuteronomy***, the main content of which is that after the Israelites left the wilderness for Canaan, Moses called unto all Israel and reiterated the commandments, statutes, and ordinances, which they were taught to observe and do when they got into the land of Canaan.

2. The Second Day (Gen. 1:6–8).

This phrase *it was good* appears on every day of creation expect of on the second day. Why?

One explanation is that the creation of water was not finished on the second day, and part was left for the third day. Another explanation is that the waters under the firmament and the waters above it were the same thing, but they were divided. That is to say, divisiveness itself was created on that day.

Here is my interpretation: In Noah's time, the waters that were divided above the firmament on the second day were poured out as rain down to the earth, and joined the water under the firmament and covered the whole world. Although it was man's wickedness that resulted in the flood, the wicked were destroyed, after all. The LORD wished the wicked to repent, not to die. *"Have I any pleasure in the death of the wicked? saith the LORD; and not rather that he should return from his way, and live?"* (Ezek. 18:23).

3. The Light without Name (Gen. 1:16–18).

① It says, *And G-d made the two great lights*; but then it refers to *the greater light* and *the lesser light*.

They both were primitively great. It was Adam and Eve's sins that disrupted this perfection, which first resulted in the moon's withdrawing itself (to be detailed in chapter 5, "Paradise Lost").

② It is well known that *the greater light* means the sun, and *the lesser light,* the moon. But why didn't the Torah explicitly use *sun* and *moon*?

The tradition explains that, at that time, the nations made and bowed down unto idols and graven images, for example, the Egyptians bowed down unto the sun. The Torah used *the greater light* to represent the sun and *the lesser light* to represent the moon lest the belief of human beings be misled.

Here is my interpretation. When the LORD created these two great lights and other stars, He didn't give names to them yet. It was later on that the LORD called them all by name. *"Lift up your eyes on high, and see: who hath created these? He that bringeth out their host by number, He calleth them all by name; by the greatness of His might, and for that He is strong in power, not one faileth"* (Isa. 40:26).

4. The Great Sea-Monsters (Gen. 1:20–21).

Since creation, the great sea-monster was alive until Jonah's time and swallowed Jonah (Jon. 1:17).

Except for the great sea-monsters, none of the names of living creatures appear in Genesis 1, why? The reason is that the LORD did not name them at that time. It was Adam who called them all by name afterward.

5. The LORD Is Omniscient (Gen. 1:26–27)

The quotation should be interpreted in combination with Psalm 139:15–16. These two paragraphs indicate that the unformed substances of human beings were made by the LORD on the sixth day. In addition, their lives and destinies were also ordained on that very day.

Everyone's life—whatever would happen to him throughout his life—was predicted at the moment of creation. His thoughts were understood, his words were heard, his deeds were seen, his experiences were known, and all were written in the LORD's book in advance.

The LORD is omniscient: before creation, He knew everything from the beginning to the end of the world. *"declaring the end from the beginning, and from ancient times things that are not yet done"* (Isa. 46:10).

6. The Eternal Sabbath (Gen. 2:1–3).

This sentence, *And there was evening and there was morning,* appear six times at the end of the first six days of creation, except for the seventh day, the Sabbath. Why?

Everything is created, including time. Along with creating the world, the LORD created time. In other words, each of the six days was itself created by the LORD. But the seventh day was an exception. It was not created, and it was just there. Before the creation of the world and time, it was there; after the end of the world and time, it will still be there. The Sabbath is eternal and outside of time continuum.

What did the LORD do before Genesis? He kept the Sabbath.

Table 3-1: Time Table of the LORD's Work

Prior to creation	Sabbath	keeping the Sabbath
1st day	Sunday	creating light
2nd day	Monday	creating the heaven
3rd day	Tuesday	creating the earth; designing plants
4th day	Wednesday	creating celestial bodies
5th day	Thursday	designing fishes and birds
6th day	Friday	designing living creatures and men and women
7th day	Sabbath	keeping the Sabbath (Gen. 2:3).

7. The First Words of the First Man

A newborn could do nothing but cry when it opens its eyes for the first time. When Adam became a living soul, he opened his eyes and saw the LORD. What was his first act?

He said: "*O G-d, Thou art my G-d.*"(Psa. 63:1)

When he saw Eve for the first time, his act was to say: *This is now bone of my bones, and flesh of my flesh; she shall be called Woman, because she was taken out of Man* (Gen. 2:23).

8. The LORD Created Animals (Gen. 2:19).

(1) What's the number of each kind of living creatures created by the LORD?

It seemed to be two, each with its mate. Actually, the LORD created the clean beasts and the fowls seven and seven, male and female, whereas the beasts that were not clean, two and two, each with its mate. This number is the same as that of each kind of animal that Noah took into the ark before the flood (Gen. 7:2–3).

(2) In what way were these living creatures brought to Adam?

All of them were brought to Adam two and two, male and female. This is exactly how living creatures got into the ark before the flood (Gen. 7:9).

9. The LORD Named the Heaven, and Adam the Earth

The LORD called the heavens all by name and taught them to Adam **(Isa. 40:26; Psa.147:4)**. Adam called all the living creatures by name **(Gen. 2:19)**. As discussed previously, a thing's name is very essential and significant. Without a name, nothing can be a real being. In this sense, Adam was the creation assistant.

10. Taming Beasts (Gen. 2:19–20).

The LORD brought *every beast of the field, and every fowl of airs* (*v.* 19) to Adam, while Adam gave names to *all cattle, and to the fowl of the air, and to every beast of the field* (*v.*20). In comparison, *All cattle* is additional in verse 20, which indicates that Adam had accomplished a significant task; taming beasts and making them cattle. Thanks to Adam, people could feed, order about, and make use of poultry and livestock like cattle, sheep, horses, and chickens. This further proves that Adam took part in creation.

11. The First Prayer of the First Man (Gen. 2:20–23)

When the LORD brought every beast of the field and every fowl of the air unto Adam, he played with them, named them, and tamed them, and he enjoyed himself. But as time went by, he noticed that all the living creatures were in pairs, the male and the female, except for himself. Adam related his loneliness to the LORD and prayed for a helper. That was his first prayer, and the LORD answered.

12. The LORD Is Omniscient (Gen. 2:18–22)

Now that the LORD intended to made Adam a helper (*v.* 18), why did He first create living creatures instead of a woman? It was only after Adam failed to find a meet for him among the living creatures and prayed for a helpmeet that the LORD created Eve. In other words, the LORD created Eve as the answer to Adam's request. Someone might ask: "So why did the LORD declare the plan prior to Adam's prayer?" The LORD is omniscient. He predicted what Adam would worry about and what he would request, so He planned in advance.

It is written, *And it shall come to pass that, before they call, I will answer, and while they are yet speaking, I will hear* (Isaiah 65:24).

Before they call, I will answer—before Adam prayed for a helpmeet, the LORD had answered it. *And while they are yet speaking, I will hear*—Adam found no a helpmeet for himself, and prayed to the LORD. As soon as he opened his mouth to pray, the LORD heard his words.

13. Abel and Cain (Gen. 4:3–7)

Why did the LORD respect upon Abel and his offering, but not respected on Cain and his offering? Some scholars explain that traditionally the LORD favored the younger son. The firstborn couldn't get his father's blessing or the inheritance.[5]

Some hold that when the LORD punished Adam and Eve, He cursed the ground. So every fruit of the ground was not clean until the flood covered the earth.

Others believe that it was not the offering, but their attitudes that made the difference.[6] Abel feared the LORD, and offered the best sheep of his flock to the LORD. Cain, on the contrary, chose the best fruit for himself, and offered the left to the LORD.

The following is my explanation: Before Adam and Eve were driven out of the Garden of Eden, the LORD called unto them and reiterated mitzvoth, and commanded them to observe and do,[7] one of which was to offer the firstlings of the cattle and the fruit of the ground to the LORD.[8]

Since Cain and Abel were children, Adam had taught them the mitzvah. Abel observed and did them all, and *offered the firstlings of the cattle unto the LORD,* whereas Cain chose *the firstlings of the fruit of the round* for himself, and offered the left unto the LORD. That is why the Torah states that the LORD had no respect for Cain who rebelled against the mitzvah, and had no respect for his offerings which were not the firstlings.

14. The Time length of Adam's Stay in Eden

How long did Adam stay in the Garden of Eden?

The "twenty-four-hours" theory dominates for centuries, in which a variety of doctrines on the good and evil of humanity have been rooted. Apparently, this theory is neither reasonable nor satisfactory. (1) How could all the events of Genesis 2-3 happen within twenty-four hours? (2) At twenty-four hours, Adam was just an infant, and it was his first time to eat of that tree. No parents would rebuke or even banish their infant from home for his first fault.

It is necessary to make clear the time length of Adam's stay in Eden, lest the LORD's attribute of mercy be questioned and the issue about the good and evil be misled.

① *And Adam lived a hundred and thirty years, and begot a son in his own likeness, after his image; and called his name Seth (Gen. 5:3).*

Adam might begat Seth not long after the death of Abel, perhaps one to two years. So it could be inferred that when Abel was killed, Adam was about 130 years old.

② *And Cain went out from the presence of the LORD, and dwelt in the land of Nod, on the east of Eden. And Cain knew his wife; and she conceived, and bore Enoch; and he builded a city, and called the name of the city after the name of his son Enoch* (Gen. 4:16–17).

When he killed Abel, Cain was not married yet, and he was young, about 20 or 30 years old. Let's take thirty. So, when he killed Abel, Cain would have been 30 years old, and Adam was 130 years old.

Thus Adam was about 100 years old when he begat Cain.

③ *And the man knew Eve his wife; and she conceived and bore Cain, and said: "I have gotten a man with the help of the LORD."* (Gen. 4:1)

Adam might begat Cain not long after he was banished from the Garden of Eden, perhaps one or two years; thus Adam was about one hundred years old when he was driven out. That is to say, Adam lived one hundred years in the Garden of Eden.

No baby can be held legally culpable. Only when he grows to an adult with sound intelligence can he undertake the due obligations of adulthood and take responsibility for his deeds. At the age of 100, Adam was an adult, and he had matured physically, psychologically and mentally, and had been familiar with the commandments, statutes, and ordinances of the LORD. In this case, he should be punished and banished once he sinned.

Enoch walked with the LORD three hundred years (Gen. 5:22), Adam walked with the LORD one hundred years, during which he was with the LORD, rejoicing and being glad.

CHAPTER 4

One Hundred Years of Glory

"O G-d, Thou art my G-d."[9]

Many years later, as he held Eve's hand and looked dully at the Garden of Eden and the tree of life from afar, Adam was to remember these words he said when he was little.

At that time, **no shrub of the field was yet in the earth, and no herb of the field had yet sprung up. But there went up a mist from the earth, and watered the whole face of the ground. And the LORD G-d formed man of the dust of the ground, and breathed into his nostrils the breath of life; and man became a living soul. He was Adam (Gen. 2:5-7).** Slowly he opened his eyes, and saw the LORD G-d. Adam was silent, the heaven and the earth were also in great silence. At last, Adam's first voice rang out: "O G-d, Thou art my G-d."

What a great a moment it was! For the first time ever, man met the LORD G-d. Just like a newborn baby was caressed by his father, Adam was born upon the side and was dandled upon the knees.[10]

1. The Grand Tour

What a brand-new world it was! The heaven and the earth were just created. It was so recent that all the stars lacked names, and in order to indicate them, it was necessary to point.

A spirit lifted Adam up, taking him away.[11] His grand tour began.

He ascended into the heavens,[12] flying in joy, in the heart of his spirit, and the hand of the LORD G-d was strong upon him.[13]

The LORD G-d showed the immense heaven to him. Adam flew around the whole solar system and then the galaxy, all over the cosmos, and he reached the edge of the heaven. In his presence, the LORD G-d introduced and called the stars all by names;[14] and not one faileth.[15]

The LORD G-d taught Adam and made him know the ordinances of the heaven, which would establish the dominion thereof on the earth.[16] Adam applauded the LORD G-d and sang to Him:

"Lord of the world, thou bind the chains of the
Pleiades, and loose the bands of Orion.
Thou lead forth the Mazzaroth in their season,
and guide the Bear with her sons!
Thou knowest the ordinances of the heavens, and
establish the dominion thereof in the earth?"[17]

After viewing the heaven, Adam entered the springs of the sea and walked in the recesses of the deep. Then the gates of death were revealed unto him. He had also seen the gates of the shadow of death[18] and made his bed nether-world.[19]

The LORD G-d shut up the sea with doors when it broke forth and issued out of the womb. He made the cloud the garment thereof, and thick darkness a swaddling band for it. He prescribed for it His decree, set bars and doors, and said, "Thus far shalt thou come, but no further; and here shall thy proud waves be stayed."[20]

After exploring the sea, Adam went back to the ground. The LORD G-d taught Adam how to determine the measures and how to stretch the line upon it, where upon foundations were fastened and how to lay the corner-stone. The morning stars sang together then, and Adam shouted for joy.[21]

Adam was led to survey unto the breadths of the earth, to know where the way to the dwelling of light and the place of darkness were. He took it to its bound, and knew the paths to its house. And he had ever entered the treasuries of the snow and seen the treasuries of the hail.[22]

The LORD G-d guided him the way by which the light was parted and the east wind scattered upon the earth. In his presence, the LORD G-d cleft a channel for the waterflood and a way for the lightning of the thunder; to cause it to rain on a land where no man was, on the wilderness, wherein there was no man; to satisfy the desolate and waste ground, and to cause the bud of the tender herb to spring forth.[23]

Adam knew who was the father of the rain, who had begotten the drops of dew, out of whose womb the ice came, and who had gendered the hoar-frost of heaven. In those days, the waters were congealed like stone, and the face of the deep was frozen.[24]

What a great tour! Adam was the unique person who knew the heaven and the earth. He marveled at whatever the LORD G-d created, and he cheered for His power and might, and he offered a hymn!

> *Praise G-d for His Omniscience*
> *O LORD, Thou hast searched me, and known me.*
> *Thou knowest my downsitting and mine uprising,*
> *Thou understandest my thought afar off.*
> *Thou measurest my going about and my lying*
> *down, and art acquainted with all my ways.*
> *For there is not a word in my tongue, but, lo,*
> *O LORD, Thou knowest it altogether.*
> *Thou hast hemmed me in behind and before, and laid Thy hand*
> *upon me. Such knowledge is too wonderful for me; too high, I cannot*
> *attain unto it. Whither shall I go from Thy spirit? or whither shall I*
> *flee from Thy presence? If I ascend up into heaven, Thou art there;*
> *if I make my bed in the nether-world, behold, Thou art there.*
> *If I take the wings of the morning, and dwell*
> *in the uttermost parts of the sea;*
> *Even there would Thy hand lead me, and*
> *Thy right hand would hold me.*
> *And if I say: "Surely the darkness shall envelop*
> *me, and the light about me shall be night";*
> *Even the darkness is not too dark for Thee*
> *but the night shineth as the day; the darkness is even as the light*
> *For Thou hast made my reins; Thou hast knit*
> *me together in my mother's womb.*
> *I will give thanks unto Thee, for I am fearfully and wonderfully made;*
> *wonderful are Thy works; and that my soul knoweth right well.*
> *My frame was not hidden from Thee, when I was made in secret,*
> *and curiously wrought in the lowest parts of the earth.*

Thine eyes did see mine unformed substance, and in
Thy book they were all written—even the days that were
fashioned, when as yet there was none of them.
How weighty also are Thy thoughts unto me, O
God! How great is the sum of them!
If I would count them, they are more in number than the sand;
were I to come to the end of them, I would still be with Thee.[25]

2. Creation of the Garden of Eden

After the tour, the LORD G-d made the earth while Adam witnessed. **And the LORD God planted a garden eastward, in Eden; and there He put the man whom He had formed. And out of the ground made the LORD G-d to grow every tree that is pleasant to the sight, and good for food (Gen. 2:8-9)** He planted in the wilderness the cedar, the acacia tree, the myrtle, and the oil tree. He set in the garden the cypress, the plane tree, and the larch together.[26]

After that, the Garden of Eden was endowed with magic and full of green grass, running streams, blooming flowers, and fragrant fruits. That was a park of pomegranates, with precious fruits; henna with spikenard plants, spikenard and saffron, calamus and cinnamon, with all trees of frankincense; myrrh and aloes, with all the chief spices.[27] **And a river went out of Eden to water the garden; and from thence it was parted, and became four heads. The name of the first is Pishon; that is it which compasseth the whole land of Havilah, where there is gold; and the gold of that land is good; there is bdellium and the onyx stone. And the name of the second river is Gihon; the same is it that compasseth the whole land of Cush. And the name of the third river is Tigris; that is it which goeth toward the east of Asshur. And the fourth river is the Euphrates (Gen. 2:10-14).**

Adam saw, and knew, and considered, and understood together, that the hand of the LORD hath done this, and the Holy One of Israel hath created it.[28]

The LORD G-d established His covenant with Adam, saying: "I am the LORD thy G-d, who brought thee out of the dust, out of ground.

> *Thou shalt have no other gods before Me.*
> *Thou shalt not make unto thee a graven image, nor any manner*
> *of likeness, of any thing that is in heaven above, or that is in*
> *the earth beneath, or that is in the water under the earth;*
> *Thou shalt not bow down unto them, nor serve them;*
> *for I the LORD thy God am a jealous God;*
> *Thou shalt not take the name of the LORD thy God in vain; for the*
> *LORD will not hold him guiltless that taketh His name in vain.*
> *Remember the sabbath day, to keep it holy."*[29]

3. The Enactment of Statutes and Ordinances

The LORD G-d took Adam, and put him into the Garden of Eden to dress it and to keep it (Gen. 2:15). The LORD G-d taught him all botany and horticulture knowledge. Furthermore, He commanded:

"When thou beatest thine olive-tree, thou shalt not go over the boughs again."[30]

"When thou gatherest the grapes of thy vineyard, thou shalt not glean it after thee."[31]

"Thou shalt not glean thy vineyard, neither shalt thou gather the fallen fruit of thy vineyard."[32]

"Thou shalt have a place also without your house, whither thou shalt go forth abroad. And thou shalt have a paddle among thy weapons; and it shall be, when thou sittest down abroad, thou shalt dig therewith, and shalt turn back and cover that which cometh from thee."[33]

"Of every tree of the garden thou mayest freely eat; but of the tree of the knowledge of good and evil, thou shalt not eat of it for in the day that thou eatest thereof thou shalt surely die." (Gen. 2:16-17)

The LORD G-d taught Adam to live perfectly. Adam followed and did exactly.

4. Creation, Name, and Domestication of Living Creatures

And the LORD God said: "It is not good that the man should be alone; I will make him a help meet for him." And out of the ground the LORD G-d formed every beast of the field, and every fowl of the

air; and brought them unto the man to see what he would call them (Gen. 2:18-19). "Hallelujah! Hallelujah! Hallelujah!" Adam cheered when he saw all these living creatures, and he played with them just as a cheerful child plays with toys.

Adam called them all by name; not one was lacking. **Whatsoever the man would call every living creature, that was to be the name thereof (Gen. 2:19).** Adam was taught biological studies on every living creature. Thus he mastered their nature and essence, classified and named them. Lo and behold, the names he called them were identical to that given by the LORD G-d (In the first stage of creation, the LORD G-d had named these living creatures and put their names in His book, which Adam was never aware of).

When they were created, such creatures as oxen, sheep, horses, and chicken were quite wild and totally field beasts. Adam was not satisfied with their habits and therefore, he domesticated them and weakened their wildness further. **And the man gave names to all cattle, and to the fowl of the air, and to every beast of the field; but for Adam there was not found a help meet for him (Gen. 2:20).**

In the Garden of Eden, Adam walked with the LORD G-d. The LORD G-d had been Adam's help, and in the shadow of the LORD G-d's did Adam rejoice. His soul clung to the LORD G-d, whose right hand held him fast.[34] Adam had stilled and quieted his soul, like a weaned child with its mother, like a weaned child was his soul within him.[35]

Every day he went out with joy, and was led forth with peace, the mountains and the hills broke forth before him into singing and all the trees of the fields clapped their hands.[36] He was filled with delight day after day, rejoicing always in the LORD G-d's presence, rejoicing in His whole world and delighting in the Garden of Eden.[37]

In addition to the relationship of the Creator and His creature, there were also three relationships between the LORD G-d and Adam.

(1) Father and son
    Adam was the child of the LORD G-d. *For thus saith the LORD: Ye shall be borne upon the side, and shall be dandled upon the*

knees (Isa. 66:12–13); and *You are the children of the LORD your God* (Deut. 14:1).

(2) Teacher and student

Adam had been well educated: ① He was taught the Torah. ② He was revealed the origin of the heavens and the earth, and all the secrets of space, land, and the underwater world. He had also learned math, physics, astronomy, geography, botany, zoology, and so on, just like Moses had learned the written Torah and oral Torah on Mount Sinai.

(3) Friends

The LORD G-d and Adam were friends, like the LORD G-d and Abraham: *But thou, Israel, My servant, Jacob whom I have chosen, the seed of Abraham My friend* (Isa. 41:8).

CHAPTER 5
Paradise Lost

1. The Sin and the Fall (Gen. 2:21–3:24)

The heaven and the earth were primitively good, both the sun and the moon were great lights.[38] In the Garden of Eden, night was as bright as day, and there was no darkness.

On a Friday one hundred years after the creation, Adam prayed for a helper.[39] The LORD G-d answered him. **And the LORD G-d caused a deep sleep to fall upon the man, and he slept; and He took one of his ribs, and closed up the place with flesh instead thereof. And the rib, which the LORD G-d had taken from the man, made He a woman, and brought her unto the man.** Adam looked her up and down and recognized that she was just what he had prayed for. "Hallelujah! Hallelujah!" He jumped with joy. **And the man said: "This is now bone of my bones, and flesh of my flesh; she shall be called Woman, because she was taken out of Man." Therefore shall a man leave his father and his mother, and shall cleave unto his wife, and they shall be one flesh. And they were both naked, the man and his wife, and were not ashamed.**

The sun was setting, the LORD G-d was about to go up from them and keep the Sabbath. Before departure, the LORD G-d exhorted them to keep the Sabbath in their house and not to leave;[40] were they to leave, the limit was not more than two thousand cubits.[41] Adam and woman promised that they would obey.

It was a charming and quiet Sabbath day: the moon was shining in the sky as it had done for the past one hundred years, and the clear sky was like a huge blue curtain hung upon the holy ark on *Yamim Noraim*.[42] Moonlight walked on the Pison, Gihon, Tigris, and Euphrates, leaving its sparkling footprints on the surface of the water. The garden was colorful and the wind brought warmth. Tree shadows swayed in the woods while leaves flashes as micro-flames. Fragrance of flowers, grasses, and fruits rippled around, giving forth an almost intoxicating scent.

Their house was on the border of the garden, and the tree of life and the tree of knowledge of good and evil were two thousand cubits away, at the center of the garden. Being just made, woman was curious about everything around. Adam reminded her of what the LORD G-d had just charged, but she did not take it to heart. For her, the glamorous garden was so fascinating that she insisted to go outside no matter how hard Adam persuaded—what is more—she asked him to go with her. Adam was too trapped to stick to the commandments. At last, he followed her.

Adam showed and told her everything: how the LORD G-d created the world and the garden; how he walked with the LORD G-d for the past 100 years. They unknowingly traveled farther more than two thousand cubits. When they passed the tree of the knowledge of good and evil, Adam was full of fear, and he repeated to her the LORD G-d's commandment—of *every tree of the garden thou mayest freely eat; but of the tree of the knowledge of good and evil, thou shalt not eat of it for in the day that thou eatest thereof thou shalt surely die.*

Under the moonlight, they wandered around—jumping and dancing like happy deer, chirping and singing like excited larks. When thirsty, they drank water from the river; when hungry, they picked fruit from trees. They viewed and admired flowers, and they teased living creatures that had still stayed at their places for the Sabbath.

The Sabbath commandment applied not only to Adam and Eve but also to living creatures. All the living creatures were resting at places of their own. **Now the serpent was more subtle than any beast of the field which the LORD G-d had made.** It broke the Sabbath commandment, wandering far and near. [43] The couple who profaned the Sabbath encountered the serpent which profaned the Sabbath.

Serpent said unto the woman: "Yea, hath G-d said: 'Ye shall not eat of any tree of the garden?'" And the woman said unto the serpent: "Of the fruit of the trees of the garden we may eat; but of the fruit of the tree which is in the midst of the garden, G-d hath said: 'Ye shall not eat of it, neither shall ye touch it, lest ye die.'" She pointed to the center of the garden, saying: "Look, it is over there."

And the serpent said unto the woman: "Ye shall not surely die; for G-d doth know that in the day ye eat thereof, then your eyes shall be opened, and ye shall be as G-d, knowing good and evil."

On hearing this, she could hardly wait to go back to that tree, but it hit Adam that something was wrong. He looked toward their house and said: "Oh dear, far away from our house! It's Sabbath today." The woman said nothing, her curiosity waxed hot. She grabbed his hand and ran. "Back please! Oh no! Back please!" he muttered, following her.

They reached the center of the garden and stood beneath the tree of knowledge of good and evil. **When the woman saw that the tree was good for food, and that it was a delight to the eyes, and that the tree was to be desired to make one wise, she took of the fruit thereof, and did eat.** Adam stared at her, "Thou … thou shalt … shalt die" he muttered in fear.

"Nonsense!" she interrupted him, "lo and behold, I'm fine." With these words, **and she gave also unto her husband with her,** picked another one, and ate, saying: "Thou hast lived for one hundred years and hast never eaten it, and, well, so sweet and delicious!"

And he did eat. And the eyes of them both were opened. To their surprise, they saw that the other was naked. They looked at each other and themselves. **They knew that they were naked; and they sewed fig-leaves together, and made themselves girdles.** That night Adam took the woman to him as wife.

When they woke up, the moon had set, and the sun was shining in the sky. They went on to wander and play as if nothing had happened …

The Sabbath passed by quickly.

The moon rose, and a new day started. Forty minutes later, the moon withdrew itself all of a sudden, and the whole world sank into darkness. "Oh dear! What happened? What's wrong?" They cried in fright. **And they heard the voice of the LORD G-d walking in the garden toward the cool of the day.** Afraid as they were, they ducked into the trees.

As for their deeds, the moon was a witness and an accomplice. It was under the moonlight that the couple left their place; it was under the moonlight that they wandered around; it was under the moonlight that they ate of the tree of knowledge of good and evil. Hence, the moon deserved punishment, but the LORD G-d did not take action because any manner of work was forbidden on the Sabbath.[44] When the Sabbath ended (forty minutes after the moon rose),[45] the LORD G-d said to the moon: "Cursed are you for their sake. Go diminish yourself. You would be saved to grow again every month." With His words, darkness fell down and shrouded the world.

After that, the LORD G-d went down to Adam's house. No one was there. The LORD G-d walked in the garden, looking for Adam and the woman. **And the man and his wife hid themselves from the presence of the LORD G-d amongst the trees of the garden.**

The LORD G-d called unto the man, and said unto him: "Where art thou?" The almighty LORD G-d knew where Adam was. His words actually meant "You were already not at the place where you should be on Sabbath."[46] He hoped that Adam would return to his house as soon as possible or at least confess. If Adam did so, he would be forgiven. Unfortunately, Adam neither returned nor repented. **He said: "I heard Thy voice in the garden, and I was afraid, because I was naked; and I hid myself."**

The LORD G-d said: "Who told thee that thou wast naked? Hast thou eaten of the tree, whereof I commanded thee that thou shouldest not eat?" Through His words, the LORD G-d reminded Adam explicitly this time: "You had eaten of the tree of knowledge of good and evil and broke the commandment." Again He gave Adam the opportunity to confess his evil and atone for it. Had he repented, He would have forgiven him for a second time. Unfortunately, Adam did not make confession again.

Adam said: "The woman whom Thou gavest to be with me, she gave me of the tree, and I did eat." It was to answer his prayer for a help that the LORD created Eve. But instead of offering thanks, Adam complained in his second reply. In a sense, he could be excused in his first reply, whereas he passed the buck in his second reply

The LORD G-d said unto the woman: "What is this thou hast done?" He turned to the woman in hope of her awakening and repenting. Had she confessed, He would have forgiven them for a third time. It was sad that she did not repent, either. **The woman said: "The serpent beguiled me, and I did eat."**

Right then, the gate of forgiveness shut, and the wrath of the LORD G-d fell upon the world. He executed judgment and punishment.[47]

And the LORD G-d said unto the serpent: "Because thou hast done this, cursed art thou from among all cattle, and from among all beasts of the field; upon thy belly shalt thou go, and dust shalt thou eat all the days of thy life. And I will put enmity between thee and the woman, and between thy sed and her seed; they shall bruise thy head, and thou shalt bruise their heel." Immediately, the serpent sloughed his skin as atonement for his sin. Since then, the serpents has shed and grown skin periodically, which is the symbol of atonement just like the moon.

Unto the woman He said: "I will greatly multiply thy pain and thy travail; in pain thou shalt bring forth children; and thy desire shall be to thy husband, and he shall rule over thee." And unto Adam He said: "Because thou hast hearkened unto the voice of thy wife, and hast eaten of the tree, of which I commanded thee, saying: 'Thou shalt not eat of it; cursed is the ground for thy sake; in toil shalt thou eat of it all the days of thy life.' Thorns also and thistles shall it bring forth to thee; and thou shalt eat the herb of the field. In the sweat of thy face shalt thou eat bread, till thou return unto the ground; for out of it wast thou taken; for dust thou art, and unto dust shalt thou return."

The LORD G-d spoke unto the couple, saying, "Ye have dwelt long enough in this garden; leave you, and take your journey, and go where you are from. Behold, I have set the land before you: go in and possess the land which I swore unto you and your seed after you."[48]

Thus saith the LORD G-d, thy Redeemer, and He that formed thee from the womb: "I am the LORD, that maketh all things; that stretched forth the heavens alone; that spread abroad the earth by Myself.[49] Drop down, ye heavens, from above, and let the skies pour down righteousness; let the earth open, that they may bring forth salvation, and let her cause righteousness to spring up together; I have created it."[50]

Thus saith the LORD, thy Redeemer, the Holy One of Israel: "I am the LORD thy G-d, who teacheth thee for thy profit, who leadeth thee by the way that thou shouldest go. Oh that thou wouldest hearken to My commandments! then would thy peace be as a river, and thy righteousness as the waves of the sea; Thy seed also would be as the sand, and the offspring of thy body like the grains thereof; his name would not be cut off nor destroyed from before Me."[51]

"Behold, I have graven thee upon the palms of My hands; thy walls are continually before Me.[52] For a small moment have I forsaken thee; but with great compassion will I gather thee. In a little wrath I hid My face from thee for a moment; but with everlasting kindness will I have compassion on thee."[53]

And the man called his wife's name Eve; because she was the mother of all living. And the LORD G-d made for Adam and for his wife garments of skins which the cursed serpent peeled off, **and clothed them.** The LORD G-d held a wedding ceremony for Adam and his wife.

2. Reiterate the Law

And the LORD G-d said: "Behold, the man is become as one of us, to know good and evil; and now, lest he put forth his hand, and take also of the tree of life, and eat, and live for ever." Therefore the LORD G-d sent him forth from the Garden of Eden, to till the ground from whence he was taken.

On their departure, the LORD called unto them and said:

"Hear, the statutes and the ordinances which I speak in your ears this day, that ye may learn them, and observe to do them. I am the LORD thy G-d, who brought you out of the dust."[54]

"Thou shalt have no other G-ds before Me. Thou shalt not make unto thee a graven image, even any manner of likeness, of any thing that is in heaven above, or that is in the earth beneath, or that is in the water under the earth. Thou shalt not bow down unto them, nor serve them; for I am a jealous G-d, visiting the iniquity of the fathers upon the children, and upon the third and upon the fourth generation of them that hate Me, and showing mercy unto the thousandth generation of them that love Me and keep My commandments.

"Thou shalt not take the name of the LORD thy G-d in vain; for I will not hold him guiltless that taketh His name in vain.

"Observe the Sabbath day, to keep it holy, as I commanded thee. Six days shalt thou labour, and do all thy work; but the seventh day is a Sabbath unto Me, in it thou shalt not do any manner of work. thou, nor thy son, nor thy daughter, nor thy manservant, nor thy maid-servant, nor thine ox, nor thine ass, nor any of thy cattle, nor thy stranger that is within thy gate; that thy man-servant and thy maid-servant may rest as well as thou. And thou shalt remember that thou were dust in the ground, and I brought thee out thence by a mighty hand and by an outstretched arm; therefore I command thee to keep the Sabbath day."[55]

"Thou shalt not murder."[56]

"Now this is the commandment, the statutes, and the ordinances, which I command to teach you, that ye might do them in the land whither ye go over to possess it—that thou mightest fear the LORD thy G-d, to keep all the statutes and the commandments, which I command thee, thou, and thy son, and thy son's son, all the days of thy life; and that thy days may be prolonged."[57]

"For the land, whither ye go over to possess it, is a land of hills and valleys, and drinketh water as the rain of heaven cometh down; a land which I careth for; My eyes are always upon it, from the beginning of the year even unto the end of the year."[58]

"Therefore shall ye lay up these My words in your heart and in your soul; and ye shall bind them for a sign upon your hand, and they shall be for frontlets between your eyes. And ye shall teach them your children, talking of them, when thou sittest in thy house, and when thou walkest by the way, and when thou liest down, and when thou risest up. And thou shalt write them upon the door-posts of thy house, and upon thy gates; that your days may be multiplied, and the days of your children, upon the land which I swore to give you, as the days of the heavens above the earth."[59]

"All the firstling males that are born of thy herd and of thy flock thou shalt sanctify unto Me; thou shalt do no work with the firstling of thine ox, nor shear the firstling of thy flock."[60]

"When ye come into the land whither I bring you, then it shall be, that, when ye eat of the bread of the land, ye shall set apart a portion for a gift unto me. Of the first of your dough ye shall set apart a cake for a gift; as that which is set apart of the threshing-floor, so shall ye set it apart. Of the first of your dough ye shall give unto me a portion for a gift throughout your generations."[61-62]

"Thou shalt not sow thy vineyard with two kinds of seed; lest the fullness of the seed which thou hast sown be forfeited together with the increase of the vineyard. Thou shalt not plow with an ox and an ass together. Thou shalt not wear a mingled stuff, wool and linen together. Thou shalt make thee fringes upon the four borders of thy vesture, wherewith thou coverest thyself"[63]

"When thou reapest thy harvest in thy field, and hast forgot a sheaf in the field, thou shalt not go back to fetch it; When thou beatest thine olive-tree, thou shalt not go over the boughs again; When thou gatherest the grapes of thy vineyard, thou shalt not glean it after thee."[64]

"Thou shalt not muzzle the ox when he treadeth out the corn."[65]

"For this commandment which I command thee this day, it is not too hard for thee, neither is it far off. It is not in heaven, that thou shouldest say: 'Who shall go up for us to heaven, and bring it unto us, and make us to hear it, that we may do it?' Neither is it beyond the sea, that thou shouldest say: 'Who shall go over the sea for us, and bring it unto us, and make us to hear it, that we may do it?' But the word is very nigh unto thee, in thy mouth, and in thy heart, that thou mayest do it.

"See, I have set before thee this day life and good, and death and evil, in that I command thee this day to love Me to walk in My ways, and to keep My commandments and My statutes and My ordinances; then thou shalt live and multiply, and I shall bless thee in the land whither thou goest in to possess it. But if thy heart turn away, and thou wilt not hear, but shalt be drawn away, and worship other G-ds, and serve them; I declare unto you this day, that ye shall surely perish; ye shall not prolong your days upon the land, which you would go into to possess it.[66]

"I call heaven and earth to witness against you this day, that I have set before thee life and death, the blessing and the curse; therefore choose life, that thou mayest live, thou and thy seed; to love Me, to hearken to My voice, and to cleave unto Me; for that is thy life, and the length of thy days; that thou mayest dwell in the land which I swore unto you."[67]

So He drove out the man; and He placed at the east of the Garden of Eden the cherubim, and the flaming sword which turned every way, to keep the way to the tree of life.

As he held Eve's hand, and looked dully at the Garden of Eden and the tree of life from afar, Adam remembered his first words: "O G-d, Thou art my G-d."

CHAPTER 6

Good, Evil and Sin

1. The Tree of Life (Gen. 2:9)

In the Eden incident, the tree of knowledge of good and evil played a prominent part, whereas the tree of life occupied too trivial a position to have any significance; it was merely mentioned in the beginning and then fades away. The LORD planted the tree of life and Adam and his wife may freely eat of it. Yet Adam and Eve turned a blind eye to it, even though it stood together with the tree of knowledge of good and evil and its fruit was close enough to touch. Their whole attention centered on the tree of knowledge of good and evil, and all their acts took place around it. As the final curtain was falling, the tree of life all of a sudden appeared: the LORD was afraid that Adam and his wife would put forth their hands and take also of the tree of life and eat, and live forever. Therefore the LORD sent him forth from the Garden of Eden to till the ground from whence he was taken, and He placed at the east of the Garden of Eden the cherubim and the flaming sword, which turned every way to keep the way to the tree of life (Gen. 3:22–24). A strange tree!

It seemed that the tree of life served to provide immortality, but it was actually not the case. Before Adam and Eve ate of tree of knowledge of good and evil, they were alive. To be or not to be did not relate to whether or not they ate of the tree of life. Even if they did not eat of it, they could still remain alive. Therefore, the tree of life was initially unnecessary and of no consequence; only when Adam and Eve ate of the tree of knowledge of good and evil did the significance of the tree of life emerge: they were about to be punished for transgressing the commandment, but if they put forth their hands and took the fruit of the tree of life and ate, they would escape from death and live forever, as shown in Table 6-1.

Table 6-1: Deeds and Fates

Deed I	Deed II	Fate
Not eating the forbidden fruit	Not eating of the tree of life	living
	Eating of the tree of life	living
Eating of the tree of life	Not eating the forbidden fruit	living
	Eating the forbidden fruit	uncertainty
Eating the forbidden fruit	Not eating of the tree of life	death
	Eating of the tree of life	Immortality

Hence, the tree of life really served to provide redemption and immortality for Adam and Eve when they had transgressed the commandments. Verily the tree of life was an atonement tree!

2. Great Is the Atonement Tree

G-d saw every thing that he had made, and, behold, it was very good (Gen. 1:31).

He hath made everything beautiful in its time (Eccles. 3:11a).

The tree of life also in the midst of the garden, and the tree of the knowledge of good and evil (Gen. 2:9).

The LORD is full of compassion and grace and mercy. He had prepared the atonement tree for Adam and Eve at least one hundred years in advance of their fall.

In traditional view, the redemption took place after the Fall, whereas in the Torah, the LORD redeemed Adam and Eve even before they broke the commandment.

In traditional view, the salvation was granted after the Fall; in the Torah, salvation was granted before the Fall.

It is also worth noting that the LORD planted the atonement tree not far off but right next to the tree of the knowledge of good and evil. Thus Adam and Eve needed neither tramp over mountains nor wade through rivers to seek it—it was close to them, just within their reach. *For this commandment which I command thee this day, it is not too hard for thee, neither is it far off. It is not in heaven, that thou shouldest say: "Who shall go up for us to heaven, and bring it unto us, and make us to hear it, that we may do it? Neither is it beyond the sea, that thou shouldest say: "Who shall go over the sea for us, and bring it unto us, and make us to hear it, that we may do it?* (Deut. 30:11–14). They didn't put forth their hands to take of it and eat, when the eyes of them both were opened, and they knew that they were naked. It was sad that they rejected the LORD's salvation.

3. The Departure and Return of Shechinah[68]

At first, the delight of the Shechinah dwelled in the Garden of Eden with Adam and Eve. The departure of Adam and Eve from their house on Sabbath evening caused it to retire from the earth to the first heaven. Eve's eating of the tree of knowledge of good and evil drove it to the second heaven; and Adam eating of the tree of knowledge of good and evil drove it farther into the third. Their failure to eat of the tree of life drove it to the fourth heaven. Adam's first failure to repent drove it to the fifth heaven, and his second failure to repent drove it farther still. Eve's failure to repent finally drove it to the seventh heaven.[69]

Then rose seven righteous men, who induced the divine glory to descend from heaven. Enoch made it descend one degree nearer. So also did Noah, Abraham, Isaac, Jacob, Amram,[70] and Moses so that the Shechinah was once more brought down to dwell with man.

4. The Day Thou Shalt Surely Die (Gen. 2:16–17)

Although the LORD forbade Adam to eat of the tree of knowledge of good and evil, Adam would not surely die even if he ate. Compare the following:

① *Of every tree of the garden thou mayest freely eat; but of the tree of the knowledge of good and evil, thou shalt not eat of it; for in the day that thou eatest thou shalt surely die* (Gen. 2:16–17).

② Of every tree of the garden thou mayest freely eat; but of the tree of the knowledge of good and evil, thou shalt not eat of it; for if thou eatest thou shalt surely die.

The second statement meant explicitly, but it is not the LORD's intention. By contrast, the first statement focuses on neither *thou* nor *eatest*, but *the day* instead. So, *In the day that thou eatest thou shalt surely die* meant the death of the day rather than the death of Adam.

A day is constituted of day and night. It was at night when Adam ate of the tree of knowledge of good and evil. The moon was made to rule over the night, and *Night* could be identified with the moon. So this statement now comes to mean the death of the moon.

As mentioned in chapter 5, the moon was the first to be cursed, and it was deprived of its brightness and died. The statement *in the day that thou eatest thou shalt surely die* was a prophecy of the death of the cursed moon.

5. Good, Evil and Sin

No doubt, good and evil is the essential issue of humanity.

(1) **Evil**
To rebel against the LORD's commandment is *evil*.

- The LORD commanded Adam and Eve to observe the Sabbath, but they transgressed. It was *evil*.
- The LORD commanded Eve not to eat of the tree of knowledge of good and evil, but she transgressed. It was *evil*.
- The LORD commanded Adam not to eat of the tree of knowledge of good and evil, but he transgressed. It was *evil*.

(2) **Good**

- To accept the LORD's redemption for the violation of commandments is *good*. For example, after Adam and Eve ate of the tree of knowledge of good and evil, it would be *good* if they could reach out their hands and eat of the atonement tree.
- To repent for breaking commandments is *good*. For example, after Adam and Eve ate of the tree of knowledge of good and evil, it would be *good* if they could repent.

Therefore, it is *good* to repent for evil and to depart from *evil*. In this sense, *good* originates from *evil*. As it states, *Depart from evil and do good* (Psa. 34:14).[71]

(3) **Sin**

Failing to do good is *sin*. In other words, it is *sin* if one neither accepts redemption nor repents when he breaks commandments.

- Adam and Eve did not reach out their hands and eat of the atonement tree. It was *sin*.
- Adam and Eve did not repent to the LORD for their *evil*. It was *sin*.

Illustration 6-1 shows the relations among *evil*, *good*, and *sin*.

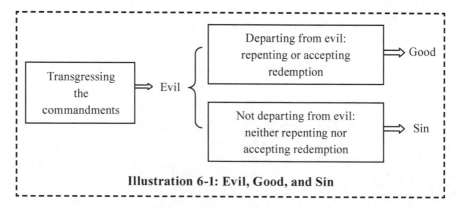

Illustration 6-1: Evil, Good, and Sin

When Adam and Eve transgressed the commandment and left their place on the Sabbath, it was evil, but not a sin. When Eve transgressed the commandment and ate of the tree of knowledge of good and evil, it was evil, but not a sin. When Adam transgressed the commandment and ate of the tree of knowledge of good and evil, it was evil, but not a sin. But their failures to seize the opportunity for redemption were sins. Yet it was not because of their evils that the LORD punished them, but because of their sins.[72]

In addition, the above relationships indicate the following (**Illustration 6-2**):

① Whether the commandments had been observed or not was the only guideline to understand and evaluate *evil*.

② Evil preceded *good* and *sin* in the Garden of Eden. Neither good and sin existed before Adam and Eve ate of the tree of knowledge of good and evil.

③ The opposite of *good* was *sin*, not *evil*.

Originally Adam walked with the LORD and lived perfectly. When he ate the forbidden fruit, Adam underwent the following transformations.

① He got a sense of shame (Gen. 3:7).

② He got wisdom (Gen. 3:6)

The wisdom mentioned here refers to the consciousness of reverence and fear of the LORD. *And he said: "I heard Thy voice in the garden, and I was afraid, because I was naked; and I hid myself."* (Gen. 3:10) Their act manifested their fear.

The fear of the LORD is the beginning of wisdom (Prov. 9:10). After Adam ate of the tree of knowledge of good and evil, the consciousness of reverence and fear developed—namely he had wisdom; before he ate of the tree of knowledge of good and evil, he had no wisdom, and he had stilled and quieted his soul; like a weaned child with his mother, his soul was with him like a weaned child (Psa. 131:2).

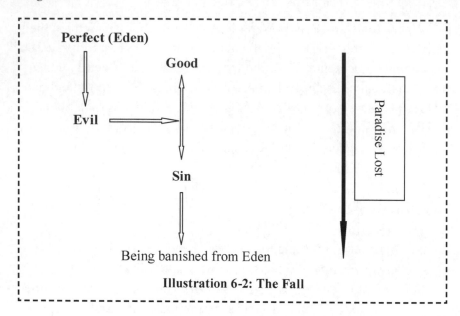

Illustration 6-2: The Fall

③ He knew the secret of the tree of life

Adam was initially unaware of the function of the tree of life had, and he might have eaten of it. When he ate of the tree of knowledge of good and evil, Adam learned the function of the tree of life: it was a tree of redemption; as long as he ate of it, he would be exempt from punishment and live forever. It was sad that Adam did not eat of it even after he knew its secret. He rejected the LORD's redemption. Instead, he figured a way to solve his problem himself; that is, he and Eve sewed fig leaves together and made themselves girdles.

④ He knew good and evil. *Behold, the man is become as one of us, to know good and evil (Gen.3:22);*

In the beginning, the consciousness of good and evil was completely foreign to Adam. But when he ate of the tree of knowledge of good and evil, Adam was all of a sudden enlightened.

- He knew that transgressing the commandment was evil.
- He knew that their departure from their place on the Sabbath day was evil.

- He knew that their eating of the tree of knowledge of good and evil was evil.
- He knew that accepting the LORD's redemption after transgressing commandments was good.
- He knew that if he could reach out his hands and eat of the atonement tree, it was good.
- He knew that if he could repent to the LORD, it was good.

6. The Righteousness and Mercy of the LORD

In Hebrew, two names are used to indicate the LORD's different attributes: *Elokim* represents the LORD's attribute of justice, and *Havayeh* indicates the LORD's attribute of mercy. Genesis 1 records the first stage of creation. In this stage, the air, sun, moon, and stars were created, which are nonliving matters. Neither mercy nor benevolence was needed with nonliving matters, so the divine name *Elokim* is used in Genesis 1 to indicate that the LORD acts in a manner of justice.

Then name *Elokim* appears in Genesis 1, while *Elokim* and *Havayeh* appear together in Genesis 2-3. Why?

(1) Genesis 2-3 records the second stage of creation. In this stage, the LORD created Adam, plants, animals, and Eve. They were living matters, and the LORD created them with His mercy and benevolence. So the name *Havayeh* is used to indicate that the LORD was acting mercifully.

(2) Although the LORD formed Adam and Eve with mercy and benevolence and had prepared an atonement tree in advance, they neither ate of the tree of life when they ate of the tree of the knowledge of good and evil, nor repented when they were asked. So, the LORD had to judge and punish them. *Elokim* is therefore used to signify the LORD's attribute of strict judgment.

That is why this dual name is used in Genesis 2-3.

CHAPTER 7
Scripture Commentary 2

1. The Micro-Torah Embedded within the Torah

In the beginning G-d created the heavens and the earth. (Gen. 1:1)

As introduced before, a micro-Torah is embedded within the Torah. The first verse, *In the beginning G-d created the heavens and the earth*, is not only the opening words of the Torah, but also that of the micro-Torah.

The correspondence between the micro-Torah and Torah are illustrated.

Table 7-1 Correspondence between Micro-Torah and Torah

Micro-Torah and its synopses	Torah and its synopses
1. Genesis 1:1–2:3 The LORD created the heaven and the earth.	**1. Genesis** The LORD created the world.
2. Genesis 2:4–14 **(1)** Originally, Adam was the dust of the ground. The LORD brought him out of the ground and formed him a living being.	**2. Exodus** **(1)** Originally, the Israelites were slaves in Egypt. The LORD brought them out of the hand of Egypt and out of the house of bondage, and made them the Chosen People.

(2) Adam was taken to visit the heaven and the earth. He witnessed also the creation of plants, animals, and Eve. He saw, and knew, and considered, and understood the power and might of the LORD.[73]	**(2)** The Israelites witnessed the chastisement of the LORD: His greatness, His mighty hand and His outstretched arm, His signs, and His work, which He did in the midst of Egypt unto the pharaoh of Egypt, and unto all his land. He made the water of the Red Sea overflow the army of Egypt, their horses, and their chariots, and He hath destroyed them unto this day.[74]
(3) The LORD commanded Adam four commandments, including the commandment of observing the Sabbath.	**(3)** The LORD commanded the Israelites Ten commandments, including the commandment of observing the Sabbath.

3. Genesis 2:15–17	**3. Leviticus**
(1) teaching Adam statutes and ordinances to perform;	**(1)** teaching Israelites statutes and ordinances to perform;
(2) preparing the atonement tree;	**(2)** instructing how to prepare a sin offering;
(3) informing of what Adam may eat and what shall not.	**(3)** informing of what Israelites may eat and what shall not.

4. Genesis 2:18–3:21	**4. Numbers**
The deeds of Adam and Eve in the Garden of Eden.	The deeds of the Israelites in the wildness.
(1) Adam numbered and named the living creatures that the LORD brought to him;	**(1)** Moses numbered the congregation as was commanded by the LORD;
(2) The couple's evils, sins and the LORD's punishment: ① They left their place on the Sabbath day;	**(2)** The Israeli evils, sins, and the LORD's punishment: ① Disaster occurred as a result of their eating of quails (11:31–34);

② They ate of the tree of knowledge of good and evil;	② The ten men who brought about the evil report died by the plague (14:36–37);
③ They failed to repent;	③ The man gathering sticks upon the Sabbath day was stoned to death (15:32–36);
④The moon was punished;[75]	④ Korah and all his company were punished because they had sinned (16:31–35);
⑤ The serpent was cursed;	⑤The plague started among the people because they complained against Moses and Aaron (17:6–15);
⑥ The ground was cursed;	⑥Miriam and Aaron died (20:1, 22–29);
⑦ The couple were punished;	⑦The Israelites died in the plague during their stay in Shittim (25:1–9);
(3) The land where they were to live was destined.	**(3)** The land of Canaan where they were to live was destined (34:1–29).
(4) The LORD made for Adam and his wife garments of skins and clothed them. Also, He held their wedding ceremony.	**(4)** As the LORD hath commanded him, Moses ordered Zelophehad's daughters to marry into the family of the tribe of their father (36:10–12).
5. Genesis (2:22–3:21) Before Adam and Eve left the Garden of Eden, the LORD called to them and reiterated the commandments, statutes, and ordinances, which He taught them to keep and to follow after getting into the ground where Adam was taken from.	**5. Deuteronomy** Before Israelites left the desert for Canaan, Moses called all Israel and reiterated the commandments, statutes, and ordinances of the LORD, which He taught them to keep and to follow after getting into the land of Canaan

2. Homosexuality (Gen. 9:21–25)

What happened after Noah got drunk? Why did Noah curse Canaan? According to the traditional explanation, when Noah became drunk and lay uncovered, Ham saw his nakedness.[76] Another explanation is that Noah was castrated by Ham. And the third one states that Ham had a homosexual relationship with Noah, or had an incestuous relationship with his mother.

In my opinion, homosexuality did happen. However, it was Canaan, rather than Ham, who did it.

①　*And Ham, the father of Canaan, saw the nakedness of his father, and told his two brethren without* (Gen. 9:22).

　　What does this phrase *the father of Canaan* mean? Why is Canaan mentioned here? Nothing in the Torah is haphazard, inconsequential or superfluous. Everything—every sentence, every phrase, and every word—is there with purpose; the appearance of this phrase *the father of Canaan* implies that when Noah was drunk and lay uncovered, Canaan did the homosexuality with Noah, which Ham ran across.

②　It was Canaan rather than Ham who had been cursed. If Canaan had been innocent, he would not have been cursed.

③　Canaan's offspring were Sodomites, who were actually homosexuals (Gen. 19:4–6).

The most grievous sin of Sodom and Gomorrah was purportedly that they prohibited people from doing good, and tortured or even killed those who did good.[77] In fact, the most grievous sin of Sodom was homosexuality. When the men of Sodom saw the angels, their evil desires waxed hot: apparently, they came for homosexuality. Lot attempted to protect his guests. *And Lot went out unto them to the door, and shut the door after him. And he said: "I pray you, my brethren, do not so wickedly."* (Gen. 19:6–7) He would give up his two virgin daughters to the Sodomites, letting them do whatever they liked with his daughters instead of his guests (Gen. 19:8). Lot would rather the

Sodomites gang-rape his daughters than have homosexual relationships with his guests, so that the angels could escape.

How exceedingly grievous the sin of Sodom was (Gen. 18:20)! Therefore it could be inferred that their ancestor Canaan was a homosexual indeed.

3. Wicked Ham

Canaan was wicked, and His father Ham too.

① He transgressed G-d's commandment when they were in the ark.

When the waters decreased, Noah and his family came out of the ark, as the Torah states: *And the sons of Noah, that went forth from the ark, were Shem, and Ham, and Japheth: and Ham is the father of Canaan* (Gen. 9:18).

Why does this sentence *Ham is the father of Canaan* appear here? What does it mean? As mentioned previously, nothing in the Torah is haphazard, inconsequential or superfluous. Everything—every sentence, every phrase, and every word—is there with purpose. This sentence *Ham is the father of Canaan* implies that Ham begat Canaan before they went out of the ark.

The LORD forbade marital relations in the ark during the flood.[78] But, Ham broke it and begat Canaan.

② He was an incompetent father.

When he ran across the wicked deed of Cannan, Ham neither reprimanded nor stopped his son.

③ He was a wicked son.

Seeing the nakedness of Noah, Ham went out to tell his two brothers instead of covering his father immediately. Ham was obviously short of respect for his father. He even shamelessly embellished and gloated at his father's nakedness.

Ham and Canaan were both wicked.

4. Righteous Shem

And he said: "Blessed be the LORD, the G-d of Shem; and let Canaan be their servant." (Gen. 9:26)

Why is Shem mentioned here with the G-d? He was as righteous and wholehearted as Noah, and observed and did the commandments, decrees, and laws of G-d.

After the flood, Noah and his family came out of the ark. *And Noah built an altar unto the LORD; and took of every clean beast, and of every clean fowl, and offered burnt-offerings on the altar* (Gen. 8:20). As for Shem, there and then he composed a hymn, known as Psalm 93.

5. The Failure of Babel (Gen. 11:1–9)

After Babel, the language of the whole world was confounded, and the people were scattered over the face of the whole earth. It is conceivable regarding how The LORD confounded human beings' language and speech: He spoke, and it was so. However, no one knows how the LORD scattered humans abroad from thence upon the face of all the earth. It is surely impossible that He put forth His hand and took them to the face of all the earth, just like He did with Ezekiel.

Now, the answer emerges: continental drift!

Continental drift hypothesis relates the topographical transformation of the earth in ancient times.[79] Originally there was only one continent on the earth, called Pangea. It was situated on the asthenosphere, the upper layer of the mantle, and was surrounded by boundless oceans, Panthalassa. As time went on, this Pangea split, drifted, and collided. In the end, the face of the earth formed (Fig. 1).

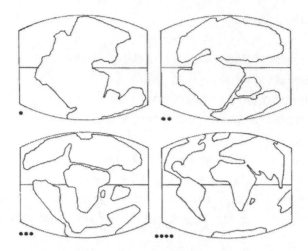

Fig.7-1 Continental Drift

Up to now, the continental drift hypothesis has been proven right by a variety of research, such as geography, geomorphology, geology, physics, paleontology, paleoclimatology, biology, etc. It was through the separation and drift of tectonic plates that the LORD scattered abroad people from thence upon the face of all the earth.

Scientists have been seeking the mechanism that caused the drift. Now the Torah gives a hint: the LORD's speech is the power.

6. The One Who Sought to Kill Joseph (Gen. 37:18–20)

And they said one to another (v. 19). It was Simeon who said these words to Levi and plotted to kill Joseph (Gen. 42:24; 34:25; 49:5).

7. Joseph's Retaliation (Gen. 42:17, 24)

They once took and cast Joseph into the pit. The pit was empty, and there was no water in it (Gen. 37:24). Joseph was trapped there three days without food and water. So, he got back at his brothers and put them all together into ward for three days.

Joseph held a grudge against Simeon who once plotted to kill him.

Recklessness of Reuben (Gen. 44:7–13).

When they were charged, a brother of Joseph swore (v. 9), which was so reckless that he put themselves at risk. It must be Reuben who said it. When he persuaded Jacob, Reuben swore on the lives of his sons (Gen. 42:37), which showed his precipitance.

9. The Wisdom of Judah (Gen. 44:14–16)

The reckless oath of Reuben put Benjamin in jeopardy. At this moment, Judah confessed their guilt and made a suggestion, astutely defusing the danger of Benjamin.

10. Jacob's Discontent with Joseph (Gen. 46:29)

The long-lost father and son finally reunited, and Jacob was both happy and disgruntled. To his joy, he finally saw Joseph again; to his regret, this reunion came too late. Because of the grudge against his brothers, Joseph made no attempt to contact his family during twenty-two years (including nine years when he was the viceroy of Egypt). When Joseph fall and weep on Jacob's neck, Jacob let him alone and had no response, expressing his discontent with Joseph.

11. Jacob's Worry (Gen. 48:5)

Simeon once plotted to kill Joseph, and Reuben once suggested casting him into the pit. Jacob knew that Joseph held a grudge against them. He feared that Joseph would take revenge on them after his death, so he highlighted the fact that Reuben and Simeon were his sons, hoping that Joseph could forgive them.

12. The Self-Introduction of the LORD

(1) *And when the LORD saw that he turned aside to see, G-d called unto him out of the midst of the bush, and said: "Moses, Moses." And he said: "Here am I." And He said: "Draw not*

nigh hither; put off thy shoes from off thy feet, for the place whereon thou standest is holy ground." Moreover He said: "I am the G-d of thy father, the G-d of Abraham, the G-d of Isaac, and the G-d of Jacob." And Moses hid his face; for he was afraid to look upon G-d (Exod. 3: 4–6).

(2) *And he went up from thence to Beer-sheba. And the LORD appeared unto him the same night, and said: "I am the G-d of Abraham thy father. Fear not, for I am with thee, and will bless thee, and multiply thy seed for My servant Abraham's sake."* (Gen. 26: 23–24).

(3) *And he dreamed, and behold a ladder set up on the earth, and the top of it reached to heaven; and behold the angels of G-d ascending and descending on it.*

And, behold, the LORD stood beside him, and said: "I am the LORD, the G-d of Abraham thy father, and the G-d of Isaac. The land whereon thou liest, to thee will I give it, and to thy seed." (Gen. 28:12–13).

These paragraphs are the self-introductions of the LORD when He appeared unto humans. It is interesting that the LORD didn't introduce Himself as the G-d of the man unto whom He appeared, but as the LORD of this man's father and ancestors.

When the LORD appeared unto Isaac, the LORD did not introduce Himself as the G-d of Isaac, but as the G-d of Isaac's father.

When the LORD appeared unto Jacob, the LORD did not introduce Himself as the LORD of Jacob, but as the LORD of Jacob's father, Abraham.

When the LORD appeared unto Moses, the LORD did not introduce Himself as the LORD of Moses, but as the LORD of Moses' father, the LORD of Abraham, the LORD of Isaac, and the LORD of Jacob instead.

To educate children is a mitzvah (Deut. 6:7; 11:9). Abraham observed it. Since Isaac's youth, Abraham taught the commandments, statutes, and ordinances diligently unto Isaac, and he told of his experience with the LORD. As a result, Isaac linked the LORD with Abraham his father.

When the LORD appeared unto Isaac for the first time, He mentioned *the G-d of Abraham your father.*

The same situation happened with Isaac and Jacob, and with Amram and Moses.[80]

Through the LORD's self-introduction, when He appeared unto humans, we can infer where their faith rooted. Whether it was Isaac, Jacob, or Moses, their knowledge and understanding of the LORD rooted in the education of their fathers until the LORD appeared and spoke with them for the first time.

However, Abraham was an exception. When the LORD appeared unto him, He did not mention Terah his father, which implied that Terah didn't teach the commandment of the LORD unto Abraham. In fact, Terah was an idolater.

13. Amram: A Righteous and Wholehearted Man (Exodus 3:6)

None of the three ancestors—Abraham, Isaac, and Jacob—succeeded in children education. For example, the LORD had no a delight in the bad character of Abraham's son Ishmael, Isaac's son Esau, and Jacob's daughter Dinah.[81] Amram, by contrast, was the most successful, and the LORD had delight in his all three children. Although living conditions in Egypt were harsh for the Israelites, Amram stuck to the mitzvah to educate children, and he finally succeeded. All his three children grew up to be the faithful and excellent servants of the LORD. Aaron became the first high priest of Israel, and Miriam was the first prophetess of Israel. Amram's three children played the most pivotal role in the event of Exodus. Amram deserved to be one of the seven righteous who had induced Shekhinah to descend from the heaven.[82]

14. Emancipation Proclamation

Part 1
Ye are standing this day all of you before the LORD your G-d: your heads, your tribes, your elders, and your officers, even all the

men of Israel, your little ones, your wives, and thy stranger that is in the midst of thy camp, from the hewer of thy wood unto the drawer of thy water; that thou shouldest enter into the covenant of the LORD thy G-d—and into His oath—which the LORD thy G-d maketh with thee this day (Deut. 29:9–11).

Part 2

And Moses commanded them, saying: "At the end of every seven years, in the set time of the year of release, in the feast of tabernacles, when all Israel is come to appear before the LORD thy G-d in the place which He shall choose, thou shalt read this law before all Israel in their hearing. Assemble the people, the men and the women and the little ones, and thy stranger that is within thy gates, that they may hear, and that they may learn, and fear the LORD your G-d, and observe to do all the words of this law (Deut. 31:10-12).

Those who escaped from Egypt were alien nobles and alien slaves as well as the Israelites. In part 1, *All the men of Israel, your little ones, your wives* stands for the Israelites, and *thy stranger that is in the midst of thy camp, from the hewer of thy wood unto the drawer of thy water* represents the alien nobles and slaves. When the Israelites escaped from Egypt, the aliens went with them and wandered together in the wilderness.

Part 2 are the statutes commanded by Moses, which they should keep after getting into the Promised Land. Compared with part 1, this phrase *from the hewer of thy wood unto the drawer of thy water* disappears, which means that when they got to the Promised Land, the alien slaves were set free.

The slave emancipation movement in America in 1863 was an epoch-making event, but it was not the earliest. The two earliest slave emancipation movements in history occurred in Egypt and in the land of Canaan. Around 1250 BC, millions of Hebrew slaves escaped from Egypt and got their emancipation and freedom. About fifty years later in 1200 BC, when the Israelites got to the Promised Land, they set free all slaves and abolished slavery in the land of Canaan.

15. The Israelites and the Nations (Num. 23:8–10)

Israelites differed from the nations in two aspects:

(1) Spatial perspective
   At the very outset of Creation, the Land of Israel was intended exclusively for the Jewish people.
(2) Temporal perspective
   Since creation, the LORD has been looking upon the world. He sees that one generation passes away, and another generation comes; and the Israelites abides for ever (Eccles. 1:4).

Franz Rosenzweig pointed out:

> *The Jew is independent from history. As an eternal nation, the Israelites are beyond history. The nations' emerging and perishing, thriving and decaying do not relate to the Israelites. Israel is neither one part of the nations, nor belongs to the world. Whatever happens in the world has hardly any value in the hearts of Israelites. The rise and fall of a country makes no difference to the Israelites. For the Jew, the world remained constant from its creation to the Advent of Messiah. They have only one mission in this world, that is, to keep their lifestyles, which are endowed with by the eternal life, to pass from generation to generation, to expect for the Advent of Messiah with hope and confidence.*[83]

16. The Israelites and the Stars in the Sky

The LORD doth build up Jerusalem, He gathereth together the dispersed of Israel; Who healeth the broken in heart, and bindeth up their wounds. He counteth the number of the stars; He giveth them all their names (Psa. 147:2–4).

The first two verses pertain to the Israelites, whereas the last verse pertains to the stars. First, the LORD took the Israelites as the stars in the sky (Gen. 15:5). Second, the Israelites were remembered and blessed by the LORD. Although they have suffered persecution and dispersion, they have never been ruined, just as the stars in the sky will never perish.

CHAPTER 8

For Thee Have I Seen Righteous Before Me

1. The Flood (Gen. 6:1–8:22)

When Noah was young, his grandfather Methuselah took him in and brought him up. Methuselah told the tales of their ancestors, taught the commandments, statutes, and ordinances diligently unto Noah; they talked about the mitzvoth when they sat at home and when they walked along the road, when they lay down and when they got up.

And it came to pass, when men began to multiply on the face of the earth, and daughters were born unto them, the sons of G-d saw the daughters of men that they were fair; and they took them wives, whomsoever they chose. And the LORD said: 'My spirit shall not abide in man for ever, for that he also is flesh; therefore shall his days be a hundred and twenty years.' The Nephilim were in the earth in those days, and also after that, when the sons of God came in unto the daughters of men, and they bore children to them; the same were the mighty men that were of old, the men of renown.

The world fell corrupt and evil. Noah attributed men's fall to their chaotic marriage, he therefore determined to keep single.

In 1536 (Hebrew calendar, about 2224 **BC**), **the LORD saw that the wickedness of man was great in the earth, and that every imagination of the thoughts of his heart was only evil continually. And it repented the LORD that He had made man on the earth, and it grieved Him at His heart.** Men made and bowed down unto graven images, committed lewdness. **And the LORD said: "I will blot out man whom I have created from the face of the earth; both man, and beast, and creeping thing, and fowl of the air; for it repenteth Me that I have made them." But Noah found grace in the**

eyes of the LORD. He walked with the LORD, observed and did the commandments, statutes, and ordinances.

The LORD appeared unto Noah and declared: "I will blot out all the flesh from the face of earth, but I will save you. Before that, you should get." Noah said: "It has been ten generations since creation. Yet despite that men have been fruitful, have multiplied, and have replenished the earth, the world degenerate. I would rather keep single lest the corruption would repeat."

The LORD hurried him into marriage and brought him forth abroad, saying: "Look now toward heaven, and count the stars, if thou be able to count them," and He said unto him, "So shall the just men of your offspring be."[84] So at the age of 480, Noah married Naamah, the sister of Tubal-cain. **These are the generations of Noah. Noah was in his generations a man righteous and whole-hearted; Noah walked with G-d.**

Twenty years later in 1556, **Noah begot three sons, Shem, Ham, and Japheth. And the earth was corrupt before G-d, and the earth was filled with violence.** Men did violence to men and made destruction of beasts. Corpses were scattered everywhere, with the blood permeating the face of the earth.

And G-d saw the earth, and, behold, it was corrupt; for all flesh had corrupted their way upon the earth. So G-d said unto Noah: "The end of all flesh is come before me; for the earth is filled with violence through them; and, behold, I will destroy them with the earth. Make thee an ark of gopher wood; with rooms shalt thou make the ark, and shalt pitch it within and without with pitch. And this is how thou shalt make it: the length of the ark three hundred cubits, the breadth of it fifty cubits, and the height of it thirty cubits. A light shalt thou make to the ark, and to a cubit shalt thou finish it upward; and the door of the ark shalt thou set in the side thereof; with lower, second, and third stories shalt thou make it. And I, behold, I do bring the flood of waters upon the earth, to destroy all flesh, wherein is the breath of life, from under heaven; every thing that is in the earth shall perish. But I will establish my covenant with thee; and thou shalt come into the ark, thou, and thy sons, and thy wife, and thy sons' wives with thee. And of every living thing

of all flesh, two of every sort shalt thou bring into the ark, to keep them alive with thee; they shall be male and female. Of the fowl after their kind, and of the cattle after their kind, of every creeping thing of the ground after its kind, two of every sort shall come unto thee, to keep them alive. And take thou unto thee of all food that is eaten, and gather it to thee; and it shall be for food for thee, and for them." Thus did Noah; according to all that G-d commanded him, so did he.**

One hundred years later in 1656, Noah made the ark. On the tenth of Cheshvan, Methuselah died. They embalmed him with grief, and he was put in a coffin.[85]

The world was down to the wire. Zeal for men ate up Noah, and he prayed, saying: "O sovereign LORD, please turn from Thy fierce wrath, and repent of this evil against Enoch's offspring."[86] And He said: "Let it suffice thee; speak no more unto Me of this matter."[87]

And he beseeched Him, saying: "Behold now, I have taken upon me to speak unto the LORD, who am but dust and ashes.[88] O Lord, will you sweep away all the living things of all flesh as the wicked? That be far from Thee to do after this manner, to slay them with the wicked, that so they should be as the wicked; that be far from Thee; shall not the Judge of all the earth do justly?"[89]

And He said: "Haven't I commanded thou that *'of every living thing of all flesh, two of every sort shalt thou bring into the ark, to keep them alive with thee; they shall be male and female. Of the fowl after their kind, and of the cattle after their kind, of every creeping thing of the ground after its kind, two of every sort shall come unto thee, to keep them alive'*?"

Noah cried unto Him, saying: "Oh, let not the LORD be angry, and I will speak yet but this once.[90] Please show your mercy and compassion upon living things of all flesh and keep them as many as those you created in the Garden of Eden—of every clean beast, seven and seven, each with his mate; and of the beasts that are not clean two [and two], each with his mate; of the fowl also of the air, seven and seven, male and female,"

The LORD then said to Noah: "thou and all thy house into the ark; for thee have I seen righteous before Me in this generation.

69

And I will hear your pray for mercy for the living things of all flesh: **of every clean beast thou shalt take to thee seven and seven, each with his mate; and of the beasts that are not clean two [and two], each with his mate; of the fowl also of the air, seven and seven, male and female; to keep seed alive upon the face of all the earth. For yet seven days, and I will cause it to rain upon the earth forty days and forty nights; and every living substance that I have made will I blot out from off the face of the earth." And Noah did according unto all that the LORD commanded him.** Besides, the LORD commanded: men and women were to live separate quarters. It's not appropriate to engage in marital relations in the ark. The animals would likewise not be allowed to mate in the ark.[91]

Noah was six hundred years old when the flood of waters was upon the earth. Noah went in, as well as his sons, and his wife, and his sons' wives, because of the waters of the flood. Of clean beasts, and of beasts that are not clean, and of fowls, and of everything that creepeth upon the ground, there went in two and two unto Noah into the ark, male and female, as G-d commanded Noah.

And it came to pass after the seven days, that the waters of the flood were upon the earth. In the six hundredth year of Noah's life, in the second month, on the seventeenth day of the month, on the same day were all the fountains of the great deep broken up, and the windows of heaven were opened. And the rain was upon the earth forty days and forty nights.

In the selfsame day entered Noah, and Shem, and Ham, and Japheth, the sons of Noah, and Noah's wife, and the three wives of his sons with them, into the ark. They carried Methuselah's coffin into the ark, too. **They, and every beast after its kind, and all the cattle after their kind, and every creeping thing that creepeth upon the earth after its kind, and every fowl after its kind, every bird of every sort. And they went in unto Noah into the ark, two and two of all flesh wherein is the breath of life. And they that went in, went in male and female of all flesh, as G-d commanded him; and the LORD shut him in.**

The flood was forty days upon the earth; and the waters increased, and bore up the ark, and it was lifted up above the

earth. **The waters prevailed, and increased greatly upon the earth; and the ark went upon the face of the waters. The waters prevailed exceedingly upon the earth;** the mountains were molten, and the valleys were cleft, as wax before the fire, as waters that were poured down a steep place[92], **and all the high mountains that were under the whole heaven were covered. Fifteen cubits upward did the waters prevail; and the mountains were covered.**

All flesh perished that moved upon the earth, both fowl, and cattle, and beast, and every swarming thing that swarmeth upon the earth, and every man; all in whose nostrils was the breath of the spirit of life, whatsoever was in the dry land, died, and their corpses floated on the surface of the water. Soon **He blotted out every living substance which was upon the face of the ground, both man, and cattle, and creeping thing, and fowl of the heaven; and they were blotted out from the earth,** the earth turned *unformed and void,*[93] none was left. **Noah only was left, and they that were with him in the ark. The waters prevailed upon the earth a hundred and fifty days.** Meanwhile, the sun, the moon, the stars and planets lost shine. The heaven and the earth were therefore plunged into a thick and dreadful darkness.

G-d remembered Noah, and every living thing, and all the cattle that were with him in the ark; and G-d made a wind to pass over the earth, and the waters assuaged; the fountains also of the deep and the windows of heaven were stopped, and the rain from heaven was restrained. And the waters returned from off the earth continually; and after the end of a hundred and fifty days the waters decreased, and the sun, the moon, the stars and planets shined again.

The ark rested in the seventh month, on the seventeenth day of the month, upon the mountains of Ararat. And the waters decreased continually until the tenth month; in the tenth month, on the first day of the month, were the tops of the mountains seen.

It came to pass at the end of forty days, that Noah opened the window of the ark which he had made. And he sent forth a raven, and it went forth to and fro, until the waters were dried up from off the earth. And he sent forth a dove from him, to see if the waters were abated from off the face of the ground. But the dove found no

rest for the sole of her foot, and she returned unto him to the ark, for the waters were on the face of the whole earth; and he put forth his hand, and took her, and brought her in unto him into the ark. And he stayed yet other seven days; and again he sent forth the dove out of the ark.

She flew straight up to Mount Zion which just emerged from the water, and the olive trees grew out of the ground there with clusters of fruits, being pleasant to the sights. **The dove came in to him at eventide; and lo in her mouth an olive-leaf freshly plucked;** so Noah knew that the waters were abated from the Mount Zion. **And he stayed yet other seven days;** In the meantime, the water decreased continually and the whole land of Israel appeared, where green grass sprouted, flowers blossomed, and various trees grew out of the ground with clusters of fruits, being pleasant to the sights. **And Noah sent forth the dove, and she** flew straight up toward Israel, and **returned not again unto him**.

It came to pass in the six hundred and first year, in the first month, the first day of the month, the waters were dried up from off the earth—from off the whole face of the earth as well the land of Israel; **and Noah removed the covering of the ark, and looked, and behold, the face of the ground was dried.** No shrub of the field was yet in the land other than Israel, but there went up a mist from the earth, and watered the whole face of the ground.

And in the second month, on the seven and twentieth day of the month, was the earth dry. On the whole face of the ground, green grass sprouted, flowers blossomed, and various trees grew out of the ground with clusters of fruits, being pleasant to the sights. **Then G-d spoke unto Noah, saying: "Go forth from the ark, thou, and thy wife, and thy sons, and thy sons' wives with thee. Bring forth with thee every living thing that is with thee of all flesh, both fowl, and cattle, and every creeping thing that creepeth upon the earth; that they may swarm in the earth, and be fruitful, and multiply upon the earth."**

And Noah went forth, and his sons, and his wife, and his sons' wives with him; every beast, every creeping thing, and every fowl, whatsoever moveth upon the earth, after their families; went forth out of the ark. Out of the ark walked Noah, trembling. He could hardly open his eyes for fear of a scarred and chaotic world with debris and corpses everywhere.

Look, a glamorous world! The clear sky was high and far, and it was like a huge blue curtain hung over the Holy Ark in *Rosh Hashanah* and *Yom Kippur*, with an arch-shaped ribbon of seven colors crossing over like a bridge. Mountains were green and the field was colorful; flowers appeared on the earth and were flourishing in full bloom. A soft breeze blew with the fragrance of flowers and fruits; the fig-trees putteth forth her figs, the olive trees bore beautiful fruits, the wines in blossom gave forth their fragrance with clusters of fruits, and the pomegranates were in flower, the mandrakes gave forth fragrance.[94]

What a brand-new world. Astonishment, excitement, and bewilderment welled up in Noah's heart, and he was unable to speak a word.

The LORD spoke unto Noah: "Behold, I have renewed the face of the earth.[101] And I have changed the earth and the heaven as a vesture, and they have passed away;[96] Now, you and your family should start a new life on this earth."

Noah builded an altar unto the LORD; and took of every clean beast, and of every clean fowl, and offered burnt-offerings on the altar. And Shem offered a hymn unto to the LORD:

Eulogizing the Majesty of the LORD
The LORD reigneth; He is clothed in majesty; the
LORD is clothed, He hath girded Himself with
strength; yea, the world is established, that it cannot
be moved. Thy throne is established of old; Thou art
from everlasting.
The floods have lifted up, O LORD, the floods have
lifted up their voice; the floods lift up their roaring.
Above the voices of many waters, the mighty breakers
of the sea, the LORD on high is mighty.
Thy testimonies are very sure, holiness becometh Thy
house, O LORD, for evermore.
—PSALM 93

The LORD smelled the sweet savour, and heard Shem's singing. **The LORD said in His heart: "I will not again curse the ground any more for man's sake; for the imagination of man's heart is evil from his youth; neither will I again smite any more every thing living, as I have done. While the earth remaineth, seedtime and harvest, and cold and heat, and summer and winter, and day and night shall not cease.**

The flood was the sole catastrophe. The LORD destroyed the wicked and the world. *I will destroy them with the earth* (Gen. 6:13). Note that the LORD didn't declare that he would destroy men "from the earth" or "on the earth", but *"with the earth"* instead, so the earth was destroyed as well. During the flood, the earth was molten (Mic. 1:4).

Actually, the impact of the flood was two-fold: destroying the world and generating a new one, with the latter more significant and profound. As the Torah states, *I have renewed the face of the earth* (Psa. 104:30) and *as a vesture shalt Thou change them, they shall passed away* (Psa. 102:26). It needs to be pointed out that *"to renew the face of the earth"* was not realized by "washing out with water." Rather, it was realized by "a new creation". In other words, the LORD first caused the world into "nothing" (naught), then brought about a new one from "nothing" (naught). When the flood covered all the high mountains, the earth melted, all the debris and corpses vanished, and the whole world turned *"unformed and void."* When the flood decreased, the LORD started to create "being" from "nothing" (naught). It was the second creation as well as a new creation. When Noah walked out of the ark, what he saw was a brand-new world.

The second creation corresponds to the first one in Genesis.

Table 8-1: Correspondence between two Creations

In the beginning, G-d created the heavens and the earth (Gen. 1:1).	In Noah's time, G-d recreated the heaven and the earth.

Now the earth was unformed and void (Gen. 1:2a).	After the flood swept and covered all the high mountains, the earth transformed greatly: the earth melted and became unformed and void.
Darkness was upon the face of the deep (Gen. 1:2b).	When the flood swept, the sun, the moon, and all the other heavenly bodies lost their shine. And the whole world was plunged into a thick and dreadful darkness.
The Spirit of G-d hovered over the face of the waters (Gen. 1:2c).	*The ark went upon the face of the waters* (Gen. 7:18b).
And G-d said: "Let there be light." And there was light. And G-d saw the light, that it was good; and G-d divided the light from the darkness (Gen. 1:3–4).	One hundred fifty days later, the sun, the moon, and all the other heavenly bodies started to shine again, and day and night began.
And G-d said: "Let the waters under the heaven be gathered together unto one place, and let the dry land appear." And it was so (Gen. 1:9).	The waters decreased continually, were the tops of the mountains seen (Gen. 8:5).
And G-d said: "Let the earth put forth grass, herb yielding seed, and fruit-tree bearing fruit after its kind, wherein is the seed thereof, upon the earth." And it was so (Gen. 1:11).	When the waters decreased, green grass sprouted, flowers blossomed, and various trees grew out of the ground with clusters of fruits, being pleasant to the sights.

And G-d blessed them; and G-d said unto them: "Be fruitful, and multiply, and replenish the earth, and subdue it." (Gen. 1:28a)	*G-d blessed Noah and his sons, and said unto them: "Be fruitful and multiply, and replenish the earth." (Gen. 9:1)*

2. Classic Questions and Explanations

(1) What's the true meaning of the verse *"But Noah found grace in the eyes of the LORD"*? Can it be regarded as a compliment to Noah?

Explanation: This verse contains a dual meaning. First, the LORD appeared unto Noah and revealed His plan to destroy the world; second, apart from saving Noah, He hurried him into marriage.

It is verse 7:1b rather than this verse that should be regarded as the compliment to Noah.

(2) *And G-d (Elokim) said unto Noah: "The end of all flesh is come before me; for the earth is filled with violence through them; and, behold, I will destroy them with the earth ... And take thou unto thee of all food that is eaten, and gather it to thee; and it shall be for food for thee, and for them."(Gen. 6:13-21)*

And the LORD (Havayeh) said unto Noah: "Come thou and all thy house into the ark; for thee have I seen righteous before Me in this generation ... For yet seven days, and I will cause it to rain upon the earth forty days and forty nights; and every living substance that I have made will I blot out from off the face of the earth."(Gen. 7:1–4)

① **Why do the two paragraphs partially repeat and contradict each other?**

② **Why does the first use the divine name *Elokim*, which represents the LORD's attribute of justice, but the second employs the name Tetragrammation, *Havayeh*, which** indicates the LORD's attribute of mercy? As for the number of animals brought to the ark, why do these two paragraphs state different totals?

③ The Torah has never praised the ancestors Abraham, Isaac, and Jacob. Why does it praise Noah especially? *The LORD said, "Thee have I seen righteous before Me."* What on earth did Noah do that the LORD praised him to his face?

Explanation:

① These two paragraphs were said at different time with an interval of 100 years. The former was said in 1556 after Noah begot three children, 100 years before the Flood; while the latter was said on February 10, 1656, the seventh day before the Flood.

② In Hebrew, two different names are used to indicate the attitudes that The LORD takes toward men. If the Torah uses *Elokim*, it means that the LORD acts with the attitude of justice toward men; if the Torah uses *Havayeh*, it indicates the LORD acts with the attitude of mercy toward men.

When the Flood was going to break out, Noah prayed for mercy and compassion for the wicked. The LORD refused. Again Noah prayed for the living things. It was the second prayer that converted the LORD's attribute from justice and wrath to mercy and benevolence. The LORD increased the number of the living things brought by Noah to the ark, from one pair to seven pairs of each kind of clean animals and birds. That's why *Havayeh* is used in Genesis 6:13–21. In other words, the former was said with the attitude of justice, and therefore *Elokim* is employed, while the latter was said with the attitude of mercy and benevolence, *Havayeh* is accordingly used.

③ Noah was kind and honest and full of love and sympathy. The LORD praised him for his prayer for all the flesh. *Thee have I seen righteous before me* (Gen. 7:1b). Someone may argue that Abraham also had prayed for Sodom, then why didn't the LORD praise him? Abraham's pray was actually for his nephew Lot rather than the wicked in the city.

(3) Why did the dove get a bitter olive leaf in her mouth (Gen. 8:10–11) **instead of a lovely and fragrant rose, or a sweet and delicious apple, or any other flower, fruit, or leaf?**

Explanation: It was from Mount Zion in Jerusalem that the dove plucked the olive leaf.

(4) The first time Noah sent the dove out, the flood hadn't decreased yet, and there was water all over. Seven days later, Noah sent her out for the second time, and she got a newly plucked olive leaf in her mouth (Gen. 8:8-11). How could the olive trees sprout and grow leaves within such a short time?

Explanation: Rabbi Levi said that the flood didn't cover Israel, and Rabbi Biryer explained that the door of the Garden of Eden was opened for the dove, from which she plucked the olive leaf. These explanations are untenable, because they contradict Scriptures.

The truth is that the LORD had recreated the world. As indicated above, as the waters decreased, the LORD initiated a new creation. The top of Mount Zion—with flowers, grass, and trees—emerged from the water. This new creation was the same as the first creation. *And G-d said: "Let the waters under the heaven be gathered together unto one place, and let the dry land appear." And it was so* (Gen. 1:9). The earth surface was uneven with mountains and grounds. In the first creation, the top of mountains first appeared from the water, and then the ground. The same was true of the second creation: first, the tops of mountains emerged, and then the ground.

The two creations differ in the speed of creation—to be specific—the speed of dry land's appearance. The appearance of the dry land in the first creation was quick —lasting less than one day, whereas the appearance of the dry land in the second creation was quite gradual—lasting 220 days from Tishri 17 when the mountains of Ararat emerged to Cheshvan 27 when the whole land became dry. This detail is shown in the following Table.

Table8-2: Process of the Second Creation

Stage	Date	Scriptures
Stage 1 The mountains of Ararat were created (without plant)	Tishri 17	*And the ark rested in the seventh month, on the seventeenth day of the month, upon the mountains of Arara* (Gen. 8:4).
Stage 2 The tops of mountains were created (without plant)	Tebet 1	*And the waters decreased continually until the tenth month; in the tenth month, on the first day of the month, were the tops of the mountains seen* (Gen. 8:5).
Stage 3 1. Mount Zion was created 2. The olive trees grew out of the ground of Mount Zion, with luxuriant leaves and abundant fruits, being pleasing to the eyes	Elul 23	*And he stayed yet other seven days; and again he sent forth the dove out of the ark. And the dove came in to him at eventide; and lo in her mouth an olive-leaf freshly plucked; so Noah knew that the waters were abated from off the earth* (Gen. 8:10–11).
Stage 4 1. The whole earth was created. 2. On the land of Israel, green grass sprouted, flowers blossomed, and various trees grew out of the ground, with luxuriant leaves and abundant fruits, being pleasing to the eyes	Tishrei 1	*And he stayed yet other seven days; and sent forth the dove; and she returned not again unto him any more. And it came to pass in the six hundred and first year, in the first month, the first day of the month, the waters were dried up from off the earth; and Noah removed the covering of the ark, and looked, and behold, the face of the ground was dried* (Gen. 8:12–13).

Stage 5		*And in the second month,*
All over the	Cheshvan 27	*on the seven and twentieth*
earth, green grass		*day of the month, was the*
sprouted, flowers		*earth dry.* (Gen. 8:14)
blossomed, and		
various trees grew		
out of the ground,		
with luxuriant		
leaves and abundant		
fruits, being		
pleasing to the eyes		

It should be noted that when the flood was decreasing, the mountains of Ararat and the tops of other mountains, though they had already emerged, were barren and without any plants. However, when Mount Zion emerged, olive trees immediately flourished there with luxuriant leaves and abundant fruits. The mountains of Ararat and the tops of other mountains, by contrast, still remained barren.

Similarly, when the land of the whole earth was created on Tishrei 1, only on the land of Israel did flowers, grass, and trees with fruits appear, whereas other lands still remained barren until Cheshvan 27.

(5) Not a single archaeological or geological evidence of the flood has been discovered yet, why?

Explanation: After the flood, the LORD had created a new world. As a result, all relics of the flood vanished. Moreover, no relics of human activities—from the Garden of Eden to the flood—were left. Neither archaeological nor geological researches about Genesis 1-11 would bear fruit, because a new earth formed after the flood.

(6) *And the LORD (Havayeh) said: "I will blot out man whom I have created from the face of the earth; both man, and beast, and creeping thing, and fowl of the air; for it repenteth Me that I have made them."* (Gen. 6:7).

Why does this verse use the Tetragrammaton *Havayeh*, which indicates the LORD's attribute of mercy, even though this verse is speaking about destruction (justice)? Whereas in another verse— *G-d (Elokim) blessed Noah and his sons, and said unto them: "Be fruitful and multiply, and replenish the earth."* (Gen. 9:1)—**it employs the divine name *Elokim,* which represents the LORD's attribute of justice even though this verse speaks of the LORD's blessing (mercy)?**

Explanation: Literally, the names the Torah uses here contradict with each other. Actually, the names are chose and used with profound meaning.

Before further explanation, we need to clarify two points. First, the attitudes that the LORD takes up toward men are classified as justice and mercy. If *Elokim* is used, it means that the LORD acts with the attitude of justice; if *Havayeh* is used, it indicates the LORD's action with the attitude of mercy.

Second, when the LORD takes up different attitudes toward men (the LORD acts with different attitudes), the fates they are to meet will accordingly differ. For example, when they commit a crime, they will be punished if the LORD takes up the justice attitude toward them and acts in a manner of strict justice. But they will be forgiven if the LORD acts with the attitude of mercy toward them. In other words, the tolerability of the LORD's mercy for crime exceeds that of the LORD's justice.

Crimes can be classified into three levels.

1. Slight crime, which is within the tolerability of the LORD's justice;
2. Serious crime, which is beyond the tolerability of the LORD's justice, but within the tolerability of the LORD's mercy;
3. Wickedness (extremely serious crime), which is beyond the tolerability of the LORD's mercy, let alone the tolerability of the LORD's justice.

In the second case, men may not get punished because the LORD still has mercy and benevolence. If the LORD's mercy and benevolence substitute for the LORD's justice at the last moment, they will be forgiven. For example, when the LORD decided to destroy the world in 1556 (verse 6:19), he initially planned to keep two of each kind of living substances, male and female. But what actually survived are fourteen of each clean animal. The reason lies in Noah's prayer for mercy for living creatures in 1656. It was Noah's prayer that converted the LORD's justice and wrath to mercy and benevolence. He altered his plan before the flood (Gen. 7:2–3).

In the third case, men are so wicked and their crimes are so severe that they exceed the tolerability of both the LORD's justice and the LORD's mercy; hence they will inevitably be punished.

Let's analyze Genesis 6:7 according to the two points above.

Havayeh was used before the verse, which indicates that "it was the merciful LORD who decided to destroy the world." In other words, "the LORD made the decision with the attitude of mercy and benevolence toward men." We can infer that "at that time, men's crimes were extremely serious that they had exceeded the tolerability of the LORD's mercy." We can further infer that "the flood was inevitable, and it is impossible for the wicked to survive."

If *Elokim* rather than *Havayeh* is used in verse 6:7, it indicates that "the LORD made the decision with the attitude of justice toward men." We can infer that "men's crimes were beyond the tolerability of the LORD's justice, but was within that of the LORD' mercy." And we can further infer that "the flood should not surely break out, because it is most likely that the LORD's mercy and benevolence will substitute for the LORD's justice at the last moment, and men will be consequently forgiven."

As mentioned above, in terms of crime, the tolerability of the LORD's mercy exceeds that of tolerance of the LORD's justice. Similarly, the blessing of the LORD's mercy exceeds that of the LORD's justice. When the LORD blesses man with the attitude of justice, the actual blessing received by man will be greater and multiplied, because most likely the LORD's mercy will substitute for the LORD's justice. The blessing given by the LORD's mercy exceeds that given by the LORD's justice. So when the LORD's mercy substitutes for the LORD's justice, the actual blessing received by man will be greater and multiplied.

Through analyzing Genesis 9:1–17 according to this principle, we can figure out:

- It is with the attitude of justice that the LORD blessed Noah and his sons.
- In reality, the LORD's mercy and benevolence most likely substituted for the LORD's justice, so the actual blessing Noah and his sons received would be greater and more multiplied.

From the analysis above, it is understandable why *Elokim* rather than *Havayeh i*s used in verses 9:1–17.

CHAPTER 9
The Story of Judah, the Hero

Chapter 38 of Genesis, which relates the story of Judah and Tamar, seems at first irrelevant and unlinked with the chapters before and after it. Most Bible critics view it as "an independent story that has no connection with the story of Joseph." On the other hand, Robert Alter explains that this chapter serves to connect Judah's deception of his father with the deception practiced on him from his daughter-in-law.[97] It is an example of the deceiver being deceived. In addition, this chapter apparently serves to emphasize Judah's negative character, adding the neglect of his daughter-in-law to his previous transgressions—betraying his brothers and deceiving his father. Mieke Bale argues that chapter 38 serves as a "mirror", a contrast to Joseph's experiences and fate. Moreover, adopting the perspective of feminist criticism, she emphasizes the role of the female character, Tamar. In her opinion, it was Tamar's behavior that helped Judah to become aware of his mistakes, resolve to mend his ways, and assume his proper household responsibilities. [98]

These approaches indicate that chapter 38 has a narrative function within the wider Joseph narrative, but far more is involved. Actually, two aspects of the chapter have been neglected: (1) its opening verse; (2) its function for the theme and motif that the whole context conveys.

Its opening verse states that *Judah went down from his brethren.* Why did he leave his brothers, and why does the Torah specifically mention this fact? The rabbis explain that *Judah went down* means that he was demoted from his precious high rank as leader of the brothers, either because he failed to prevail on them to rescue Joseph (*Midrash Tanhuma, Vayeshev 12*) or because his own rescue attempt was incomplete (TB Sotah 13b). The theme of these explanations is that while Judah acted commendably by persuading his brothers to sell Joseph rather than leave him to die in a pit, more was expected of him. He did not live up to his potential ability as a leader and positive influence. R. Abraham Saba

(1440-1508), in his *Tzeror ha-Mor* commentary, maintained that Judah was behaving like a penitent: he moved away from his brothers so as to distance himself from their negative influence, or else he could not bear to see his father's agony over the loss of Joseph, knowing that he was to blame. Kimhi (Radak) notes that Adullam, where Judah camped, is geographically south of Dotham, where the brothers were pasturing their flock in the previous chapter (Gen 37:17), thus *Judah went down* means that he traveled south. Note that while Judah's brethren did not treat Joseph as a brother, due to the favoritism shown him by Jacob and probably because they had different mothers, Judah explicitly called Joseph as *"our brother, our own flesh and blood"* (Gen. 37:27). On this basis, I think that Judah probably followed the Ishmaelites' path and headed south till Adullam, endeavoring to track them down in the hope of finding Joseph and bringing him back to their father. To his disappointment, Joseph had never been heard from since. What happened afterward is put down in chapter 38. In fact, during those years in Adullam, Judah constantly looked for Joseph.

Chapters 37–50 of the book of Genesis are generally viewed as "the story of Joseph." But it actually has dual narrative framework: it is also "the story of Judah", of which chapter 38 forms part. The narrative framework presents two concurrent stories of growth and change, featuring both Joseph and Judah. In other words, its narrative frame is like an ambiguous figure; in an ambiguous figure, objects are organically integrated by being each other's background, for example, painting "Vase and faces" [99] has two objects in it: a white vase can be made out should the dark parts be treated as the background, and two dark faces should the white part be treated as the background. In painting "Knights," [100] white knights and black knights are heading in opposite directions, being each other's background.

Throughout chapters 37–50, "the story of Joseph" and "the story of Judah" are skillfully intermingled to form a harmonious, integrated narrative framework. There are two storyline, one focusing on Joseph's behavior and the other on Judah's development as a leader. Of course, the storyline about Joseph is more prominent and explicit, while the one concerning Judah is mainly implied.

Joseph obviously hated his brothers for what they did to him, which explained why he made no attempt to contact his family after becoming viceroy of Egypt. Yet Jacob, his father, never did him any harm; on the contrary, Jacob loved Joseph and set him above his brothers. Jacob was heart-stricken when he learned of Joseph's supposed death, as the Torah puts it:

Then Jacob tore his clothes, put on sackcloth and mourned for his son many days. All his sons and all his daughters rose up to comfort him; but he refused to be comforted; and he said: "Nay, but I will go down to my son mourning." And his father wept for him (Gen. 37:34–35).

Jacob constantly bewailed him, and suffered misery and torment ever after. Joseph's failure to contact Jacob, who was innocent of any wrongdoing, may be seen as a rejection of filial responsibility.

The names Joseph gave his two sons reveal what was on his mind. Manasseh was so named because *"for G-d hath made me forget all my toil, and all my father's house"* (Gen. 41:51), and Ephraim because *"for G-d hath made me fruitful in the land of my affliction"* (v. 52). Together, these names point to a repudiation of his family and past and to the joy of his well-being in Egypt.

Joseph had little regard for the plight of his kinsfolk during the time of regional famine. When the LORD allow Joseph to foresee the seven years of abundance and seven years of scarcity, he collected all the food of those abundant years on Pharaoh's behalf, but gave no thought to his own father and brothers. When the good years had passed and the years of famine arrived, he opened all the storehouses and sold grain to the Egyptians, but evidently showed no concern for his family in Canaan. Joseph may conceivably have expected their arrival in Egypt to purchase food, this being part of some master plan he had devised, but there is nevertheless an element of callousness in his behavior. Even after Joseph encountered his brothers, he hid his true identity from them and seemed only to concern himself with the fate of Benjamin. His original idea, it appears, was only to make sure that Benjamin, his brother by blood, would enjoy the good life with him in Egypt. Joseph seems apathetic, narrow-minded, and selfish, as in his youth.

While Joseph was intent on subjecting his brothers to a series tests and trials, it was Judah who brought a positive denouement to the story.

He thus maintained his role of savior as in previous critical situations. When Joseph was in danger, it was Judah who saved him (Gen. 37:18–28). The brothers plotted to kill Joseph and Reuben suggested that they throw him into an empty pit. Since it was too deep for him to climb out, Joseph would be exposed to the burning sun by day and to the freezing cold by night. He would probably die there, but (as Reuben explained to his brothers) they would not have his blood on their hands (Gen. 37:22). Although they witnessed Joseph's anguish and heard him plead for his life, none of them paid heed (42:21) except for Reuben—who meant to release him from the pit when no one else was around (37:21-22, 29-30)—and Judah, who spotted at an Ishmaelite caravan heading for Egypt, then thought of a way to save Joseph's life (37:26-27) and so, accidently, made him destined for greatness. Judah could have done more to rescue Joseph, but his own career as a leader now began.

Later, when the whole family was starving, and the brothers could find no way to obtain food other than by returning to Egypt with Benjamin, it was Judah who saved the day. Although Rueben offered his two sons' lives as collateral for Benjamin's safe return, Jacob still refused to have Benjamin taken to Egypt (Gen. 42:37-38). They had thus reached an impasse. It was Judah who solved the problem by persuading Jacob to agree. Unlike Reuben, who offered his two sons' lives as security, Judah made himself responsible for Benjamin's safety, a more ethical proposal, and this touched Jacob's heart-strings (Gen. 43:9-11).

Finally, when Benjamin was taken to Egypt and detained there as an alleged thief, it was again Judah who saved him (Gen. 44:18–34). Judah's emotional but well-argued appeal to Joseph stressed the fact that Joseph and Benjamin were Jacob's favorites (*v.* 27) and that his own life was bound up with Benjamin's (*v.* 20-31). On hearing this, Joseph could no longer control himself; he wept aloud and then made himself known to his dumbfounded brothers (45:1-3). Joseph now realized how greatly Jacob cherished Benjamin and himself, and how sincerely Judah loved Benjamin and their aged father. Judah's moving speech, his self-sacrificing readiness to free Benjamin, and his exemplary courage made a deep impression on Joseph and his brethren. The hatred he felt for them was at last dispelled, giving way to affectionate reconciliation, and Joseph brought his family to live in Egypt.

Chapters 37-50 of Genesis show that the fate of Joseph and his family was changed by Judah. He, rather than Joseph, was the true hero of this story. It was Judah who saved Joseph's life, who secured grain for his family by persuading Jacob to send Benjamin with him to Egypt, who volunteered to sacrifice himself for Benjamin, and who brought about the reconciliation through his impassioned plea. Joseph responded by supplying wagons to bring his family from the hardships of Canaan to the comforts of Egypt. How did Judah transform himself from the failed rescuer of chapter 37 into the selfless leader of chapter 44? That is explained in chapter 38, which fits organically into the whole scenario, allowing us to observe Judah's developing sense of leadership and responsibility. He at first ignores his daughter-in-law's plight, but by the end of the episode he admits that he was wrong and had not lived up to his responsibilities (Gen. 38:26). When his shameful behavior is exposed and he is thoroughly discredited, Judah makes no attempt to obscure or deny his culpability. Instead, he bravely acknowledges it and repents. Having learned the lesson of his earlier failure to save Joseph, he must now assume the mantle of a responsible leader and do what is right, even when it is hard for him. This chapter marks a turning point in Judah's life, after which the narrative shows him leading his brothers in a proper and successful way.

Later, when Jacob gathers his sons together before his death, giving each of them his evaluation and prediction (49:8-12), Judah receives an accolade higher than those awarded to Joseph and his other brothers, for Judah will become their leader and rule Israel (*v.*8). An interesting and dramatic feature here is Jacob's prediction: *Your father's sons shall bow down before you*, an omen in Joseph's dreams (37:6-9), is now attached to Judah. Jacob chooses it for Judah when he blesses to his sons, even though Joseph, not Judah, is viceroy of Egypt at the time. It signifies that authority will be transferred from Joseph to Judah.

The scepter shall not depart from Judah, nor the ruler's staff from between his feet; so that tribute shall come to him and the homage of peoples be his (49:10). The Chosen People have two designations: Israel and the Jews. The name "Jew" comes from Jacob's fourth son Judah, rather than Reuben, Joseph or the other sons. As history has shown, Judah and his heirs played a leading role in the development of the

Israelites. Judah's tribe headed all the others and his descendants, from King David onwards, were the nation's rulers.

Chapters 37-47 of Genesis are widely regarded as the "Joseph Narrative," and Joseph did appear in them as the leading figure. However, the person who underwent a real transformation and development of character, emerging as the active hero of those chapters, was in fact Judah.

CHAPTER 10
Now Therefore Go, Moses!

1. Concealing Identity (Exod. 2:16–20)

Since he escaped from Egypt, Moses had concealed his identity out of fear. When he met the daughters of the priest of Midian, he lied that he was an Egyptian, and they trusted his words. His true identity and his experiences in Egypt were therefore kept secret until he returned to Egypt afterwards.

2. The Bush (Exod. 3:1–2)

Why did The LORD appear unto Moses in the bush instead of in another place—for example, on a high mountain or under a giant tree? Unlike mountains and trees where people and animals can get, bushes are rarely trodden underfoot by people or animals, because there are full of thorns! Ever since creation, neither people nor animals got close to that bush at Horeb, with no footprint of men or animals left, so it was a holy and pure ground.[101]

3. Lengthy Delay in Midian (Exod. 4:18–20)

There was a long interval of time between verses 18 and 19. When Moses asked for a departure, Jethro consented instantly, but Zipporah refused. So Moses had to remain in Midian. In the meantime, Zipporah bore their second son.

Verse 19 happened after the birth of their second son. This time, Zipporah agreed to Moses' request. However, she asked to bring the children with him, so Moses set out with the whole family.

4. Now Therefore Go, Moses!

And it came to pass on the way at the lodging-place, that the LORD met him, and sought to kill him. Then Zipporah took a flint, and cut off the foreskin of her son, and cast it at his feet; and she said: "Surely a bridegroom of blood art thou to me." So He let him alone. Then she said: "A bridegroom of blood in regard of the circumcision." (Exod. 4:24–26)

The verses above, judged either literally or from their content, seem more an independent part that is irrelevant from the rest of the context. They are extremely mysterious in the Torah: ① why did the LORD seek to kill Moses on the way for his mission? What was Moses' error? ② why was he saved after Zipporah circumcised their son, and how did she know this remedy?

Traditionally, it is considered that this short story, a fragment of earlier material, was awkwardly inserted into the text by the compiler of the Torah, which detracts from the integrity of content and the fluency of narration. The common explanation goes like this: the LORD got angry because Moses took his task too urgently to circumcise his son, which was required as an Israeli father's duty.[102] Talmud states that the circumcision is so essential that every pious and faithful man such as Moses and Abraham should do it without any delay, so as to be identified as "a whole-hearted man."

But other scholars hold that Moses's error lay in delay rather than hurry. He delayed at the lodging place rather than hurrying to Egypt.[103]

The story goes on like this.

After Zipporah gave birth to the second son, the LORD informed Moses that the pharaoh who sought to kill him had already died, and hastened his return to Egypt. With the consent of his wife, Moses set out with the whole family. At that time, unaware of the real purpose of Moses's journey to Egypt, Zipporah believed that he went back just to visit his brother, which was what Moses said (Exod. 4:18). Furthermore, Zipporah was unaware that he was a Hebrew because he had concealed his true identity as well as the real cause that he left Egypt.

On the way to Egypt, Moses became more and more stressed and overwhelmed. ① He panicked that he would surely be killed by the Pharaoh. Though the LORD had promised nine times to help him, he remained doubtful. ② He felt guilty that Zipporah had been kept in the dark about all the truth. ③ He was bewildered about when and how he should confess the lies to her.

The day was declining when they passed Mount Sinai, they settled down for the night and would set out the second day. **And it came to pass on the way at the lodging place,** thinking again and again, Moses eventually plucked up the courage to come clean. Never had she recognized that her husband, the man who had lived with her for forty years, was a Hebrew and the onetime Egyptian prince, nor had she ever realized that he was wanted by the pharaoh, and still never had she been aware that his visit to Egypt this time was to free the Hebrew slaves. Zipporah was so staggered that she almost fell flat on her back when Moses stammered out the truth! When she managed to regain control of herself, fright gave place to wrath. Screaming and crying, she insisted on return. Stuck in her ranting, Moses wavered again, and he had to comply. During their forty years of marriage, Ziporrah used to make the decision on every affair, and Moses was used to follow. In fact the first time Moses asked to go to Egypt, it was Zipporah's dissent that aborted the plan.

The whole family scrambled to pack up and turn back. Lo and behold, Mount Sinai was altogether on smoke, the LORD descended upon it in fire; and the smoke thereof ascended as the smoke of a furnace, and the whole mount quaked greatly.[104] The LORD appeared!

The LORD met him on their way turning back, **and sought to kill him.** The LORD lifted Mount Sinai over them like an [inverted] barrel and said: "If you go, all will be well; but if not, this will be your burial place" Right then, there were thunders and lightnings and a thick cloud upon the mount, and the voice of a horn exceeding loud.[105] And the whole family trembled. They had no choice but to submit.

And lo Zipporah cried unto the LORD. She beseeched Him for a covenant for Moses' safety in Egypt. The LORD answered her. Moses and Zipporah needed to kill a beast and sprinkle the blood onto their bodies for the covenant (Exod. 24:8). However, at that place and that moment, no beast was available. How should they do it? Zipporah hit on a solution the moment she caught sight of her sons—circumcision!

It was of great importance for the Hebrew to circumcise their newborn babies. When in Midian, Moses had concealed his true identity, and his two sons were not yet circumcised. Zipporah was about to circumcise them, which would serve to not only fulfill Moses' task as a Hebrew father but also offer the blood for the covenant.

Then Zipporah took a flint, and cut off the foreskin of her son, and cast it at his feet [symbolizing the blood was sprinkled on Moses]; **She said, "surely a bridegroom of blood art thou to me," and so He let him alone.** Zipporah was sure that the covenant took effect, and that Moses would go and return in peace. **Then she said: "A bridegroom of blood in regard of the circumcision."**

And it came to pass after this thing, Moses sent away Zipporah and his sons,[106] and he went to Egypt himself.

5. Moses's Ten Evasions

The event of Exodus was of great significance in not only Hebrew history but also human history. The whole course was tortuous and thrilling. The pharaoh at first refused to hearken unto the request and command of Moses and Aaron. He hardened his heart and refused time and time again, while the LORD multiplied his signs and wonders time and time again. Not until all the firstborn of both men and beasts were slain did the pharaoh surrender. Moses struggled with the pharaoh ten times.

Initially, Moses evaded the LORD's call. He was so afraid that he evaded and declined while the LORD persuaded, encouraged, and even promised him time and time again. Not until he was going to be killed did Moses hearken unto the LORD. Ten times he evaded and declined.

Table 10-1: Moses' Evasion

	Moses' Evasions	The LORD's Persuasion, Encouragement, Promise, and Warning
1st time	*Who am I, that I should go unto Pharaoh, and that I should bring forth the children of Israel out of Egypt?* (Exod. 3:11)	*Certainly I will be with thee* (Exod. 3:12)
2nd time	*They shall say to me: 'What is His name?' what shall I say unto them?* (Exod. 3:13)	*And God said unto Moses: "I AM THAT I AM" and He said: "Thus shalt thou say unto the children of Israel: I AM hath sent me unto you."* (Exod. 3:14)
3rd time	Declining	Enlightening him again about His great name: *"This is My name for ever, and this is My memorial unto all generations."* (Exod. 3:15)
4th time	*They will not believe me, nor hearken unto my voice; for they will say: 'The LORD hath not appeared unto thee?'* (Exod. 4:1)	Bestowing him with the first wonder: the staff became a snake, then a staff again (Exodus 4:2–4)
5th time	Declining	Bestowing the second wonder: the hand became leprous, and then recovered (Exod. 4:6–7)
6th time	Declining	Bestowing the third wonder: *"The water which thou takest out of the river shall become blood upon the dry land."* (Exod. 4:9)

7th time	*"Oh Lord, I am not a man of words, neither heretofore, nor since Thou hast spoken unto Thy servant; for I am slow of speech, and of a slow tongue."* (Exod. 4:10)	*"Now therefore go, and I will be with thy mouth, and teach thee what thou shalt speak."* (Exod. 4:12)
8th time	*"Oh Lord, send, I pray Thee, by the hand of him whom Thou wilt send."* (Exod. 4:13)	Assigning Aaron as his assistant (Exod. 4:14–16)
9th time	Lengthy delay in Midian.	*"Go, return into Egypt; for all the men are dead that sought thy life."* (Exod. 4:19)
10th time	Turning back on the way to Egypt	*The LORD met him, and sought to kill him* (Exod. 4:24)

That night the LORD gave Moses stern warning, commanding him to execute his mission. "Now therefore go, Moses!" the LORD called.

Therefore, Moses went valiantly to Egypt. The scene of the Mount Sinai burning and hanging overhead remained engraved in his mind, and it never vanished ever since. Moses was never cowardly and wobbling no matter how hard the later tests were.

6. Saving the Default People (Exod. 32:19; *Deut. 9:15–17*)

Why did Moses cast the tables out of his hands and break them beneath the mount immediately after he caught sight of the calf and the dancing? It was to save his people that Moses did so.

Moses was fearful and angry when he saw the calf and the dancing. What enraged him was that they bowed down unto the molten calf of gold and had transgressed the covenant. What scared him was that they would surely get punished for their breach of the covenant.

Not to make and bow down unto any graven images was what the LORD had commanded on Mount Sinai (Exod. 20:4–5), and all the people had seen and heard (Exod. 20:19–23), and they promised to do the commandment (Exod. 24:3). At last, on behalf of all the people, Moses held a covenant ceremony (Exod. 24:6–8), and his acceptance of the tables of the covenant symbolized that the covenant had came into effect.

The congregation had broken the covenant in that they bowed down unto the calf of gold. According to the covenant, the LORD would curse and punish the disobedient. The tables were the symbol of the covenant, and Moses broke them instantly with the purpose of tearing up the covenant. In this way, he attempted to terminate (invalidate) the covenant by himself so that the congregation could avoid the liability for the breach of covenant and therefore escape from punishment.

Though breaking the tables and tearing up the covenant might enrage the LORD, Moses did it without any hesitation. He would be punished himself for terminating the covenant rather than the congregation being punished for violating the covenant.

It was out of love that Moses broke the tables so as to save his people.

7. Profaning the Sabbath (Num. 20:10–11)

What the LORD commanded Moses was to *"speak ye unto the rock before the people's eyes"* (v. 7–8). Nevertheless, what Moses actually did was to smite the rock with his rod twice (v. 11).

It was the Sabbath that day!

According to the mitzvah, no work was permitted on the Sabbath. "Speaking to the rock" was not a work, but "smiting the rock" was. Apparently, Moses profaned the Sabbath. So the LORD punished him. *And the LORD said unto Moses and Aaron: "Because ye believed not in Me, to sanctify Me in the eyes of the children of Israel, therefore ye shall not bring this assembly into the land which I have given them"* (Num. 20:12).

CHAPTER 11

From Eden to China

What was the tree of knowledge of good and evil? Which fruit did it produce, or was it merely a symbol?

The Torah doesn't reveal this to us. Being the most famous riddle, it has puzzled people for thousands of years. Behold, it is going to be brought to light. It is concealed in a Chinese character. Furthermore, many Chinese characters contain the meanings highly consistent with the record of Genesis.[107]

China and Israel are thousands of miles apart, with very different languages, cultures, and religious beliefs. How could they relate to each other?

It traces back to Adam.

Although Adam was driven out of the Garden of Eden, his experience and knowledge in the garden remained engraved on his memory. He recounted them to his son Seth, and Seth to Enos. In this way, the messages had been handed down orally from generation to generation. After the Babel incident, humans were scattered abroad upon the face of all the earth. The people who immigrated to China still preserved the oral message, and infused them into the characters they made. Over the course of time, oral messages did not pass down anymore and faded away. Nonetheless, the characters they made have been speaking silently volumes about the remote memories.

From Chinese characters, people can obtain the primary memory about creation and the Eden incident. They can also realize Chinese ancestors' instructions and teachings contained in one character after another. Chinese characters are hieroglyphics to express meanings, as well as ancient Egyptian, Sumerian and Mayan words. For example: the character to mean "mouth" was initially written as ♡, which had a mouth shape. Over time, ♡ transformed into 口. Besides of "mouth," 口 refers to activities with mouth, like "eating," "saying," and so on.

The Chinese character to mean "tree" was primitively written as 朩, which had a tree shape. After years, 朩 transformed into 木. In addition to the meaning of "tree", 木 also has extended meanings such as "fruit" and "fruiter".

1. 造 (create, creation)

In Hebrew, *bara* means "create" and "creation". It represents in particular the behavior of the LORD. In Chinese, 造 means "create" and "creation". Its structural feature is in accord with the record of creation in the Torah.

Throughout the account of creation, everything was brought into being through the LORD's speaking while His Spirit was moving. Thus the creation has two characteristics: ① motion: *The spirit of G-d moved upon the face of the waters*; and ② speech, proclaiming, "G-d said . . ." (The phrase *G-d said* appears nine times in the account of creation.)

The character 造 exactly contains these two characteristics. The structure of 造 from left to right consists of 辶 and 告 (造=辶+告); 辶 means "motion, move," and 告 means "proclaim, speech."

```
造   =   辶   +   告
create,   move,   proclaim,
creation  motion   speech
```

Obviously, the ancient Chinese knew the story of creation. So, they made 造 according to their knowledge.

2. 明 (bright, brightness)

And G-d made the two great lights (Gen. 1:16).
This verse implies that both the sun and the moon were primitively bright. Before the Fall, the world was perfect, and the sun and the moon had the same brightness.[108]

The character 明 consists of two parts: 日 is on the left, which means "the sun", while 月 is on the right, which means "the moon" (明=日+月).

```
明  =  日  +  月
bright   sun    moon
```

Apparently, the structure of 明 is consistent with the record of the Torah and confirms our previous interpretation.

3. 梦 (dream)

The character 梦 means "dream." This character is composed of three parts from left to right and from top to bottom: 木, 木, and 夕 (梦=木+木+夕). As mentioned before, 木 means "tree," two appearances of 木 stand for the two trees in the Garden of Eden. 夕 represents "night," when one is asleep and dream.

```
梦   =   木    +    木    +   夕
dream,    the tree    the tree      night
to dream   of life     of good
                       and evil
```

As an ancient saying goes, "the day has thoughts; the night has a dream." That two trees were so impressive to the ancient Chinese that two 木 were utilized to form the character 梦, through which they hoped that the offspring would learn the lesson of the Eden incident.

4. 思, 想 (ponder, think, desire)

思 and 想 are synonyms that stand for psychological activities, for example, "think," "yearn for," "ponder," "reflect on" and so on.

The character 思 is constituted of two parts: 田 on the top and 心 on the bottom. 田 part means "garden," "orchard," or "field." Here, it specifically stands for the Garden of Eden. 心 means "heart." (The ancient Chinese believed "heart" was the physical organ to think, miss, reflect on, or analyze).

思 ＝ 田 ＋ 心

思	=	田	+	心
ponder, think, reflect on		garden of Eden		heart

Making 思 in this way, the ancient Chinese hope offspring could always think over and reflect on what happened in the Garden of Eden.

The character 想 comprises three parts from left to right, and from top to bottom: 木, 目, and 心 (想=木+目+心). 目 means "eyes," and has the extended meaning, such as "stare," "watch," "look," "see" etc. As mentioned before, 木 means "tree," in this case particularly means the tree of knowledge of good and evil. 心 means "heart."

想	=	木	+	目	+	心
think, ponder, yearn for		the tree of good and evil		stare at, look at, watch		heart

Thus, 想 contains such instructions as "to remember, ruminate and reflect on the tree of good and evil".

5. 要 (desire, ask for)

Adam's first prayer was to ask for a help. The LORD answered him, and created and brought Eve to him. The character 要 means "desire," "ask for," "request," "require," etc. It consists of two parts: 西 on the top and 女 on the bottom. 西 means "west," "western," 女 means "woman," "women."

```
要  =  西  +  女
desire,    west,    woman,
ask for   western   women
```

The Garden of Eden lay to the west of China. Therefore, "western woman" (the woman in the west) stands for Eve. The character 要 indicates that Eve was what Adam desired and prayed for.

6. 它 (it)

Now the serpent was more subtle than any beast of the field which the LORD G-d had made (Gen. 3:1).

In Chinese, 它 means "it." The original form of 它 is written as 𠃊. In the Eden incident, serpent is the sole living creatures that transgressed the Sabbath and tempted Eve to eat the fruit from the tree of knowledge of good and evil. So when the ancient Chinese came to made a character to represent the third-person "it," they chose the shape of the serpent (𠃊) instead of the shape of other animals, like bird (🐦), sheep (🐑), or oxen (🐂).

7. 气 (breathe, life) ; 乞 (seek, long for); 吃 (eat)

Then the LORD G-d formed man of the dust of the ground, and breathed into his nostrils the breath of life; and man became a living soul (Gen. 2:7).

(1) The original form of 气 (breathe, life) was ⟨image⟩. It was a pictograph showing the track of *"breathed into his nostrils the breath of life,"* in which the side lines stood for Adam's respiratory tract and the middle line represented the breathing path of the breath.

101

(2) Another character, 乞 (seek, ask for) was made on the basis of 气. In comparison, the structure different between 气 and 乞 lies in the middle line "—" of 气, which 乞 lacks. As mentioned above, the "—" in 气 stands for "the breath of life from the LORD."

乞 + — = 气

乞		—		气
seek, ask for		the breath of life from G-d		life, breath

Many matters, such as money, gold, silver, bread, food, and so on, are sought and longed for by everyone. Nevertheless, from the perspective of the ancient Chinese, these matters were not the most valuable.

The difference between 气 and 乞 conveys the teaching that the spirit and life from the LORD were the most worth seeking and longing for. With it, people would have life, whereas people without it should long for and try hard to seek it.

(3) 吃 (eat, feed) is made up of two components: 口 (mouth, eat) on the left, and 乞 (seek, ask for) on the right.

Apparently, the structure of 吃 is unrelated to food or bread, and is related to "seek, long for (乞)" instead. As analyzed above, 乞 contains the teaching that the Holy Spirit and life from the LORD are the most worth seeking.

吃 = 口 + 乞

吃		口		乞
eat, feed		mouth,		seek, ask for

Therefore, 吃 contains the following instruction: whenever one eats, he (she) should remember that it is the holy spirit and life breathed by the LORD, rather than bread, that are the most essential and worth seeking. Whenever one eats, he (she) should ruminate on the verse: *man doth not live by bread only, but by everything that proceedeth out of the mouth of the LORD doth man live* (Deut. 8:3b).

8. 罪 (sin, crime)

The character 罪 (sin, crime) consists of two parts: 四 (four, four times) and 非 (error, wrong).

罪	=	四	+	非
sin, crime		four, four times		error, wrong

The LORD is compassionate and gracious, slow to anger, abounding in love (Psa. 103:8). But after seven consecutive errors of Adam and Eve, the LORD punished them. These seven errors were: ① they left their place at Friday night; ② Eve ate of the tree of knowledge of good and evil; ③ Adam ate of the tree of knowledge of good and evil; ④ they did not eat of the tree of life; ⑤ Adam did not confess in his first reply; ⑥ Adam did not confess in his second reply; ⑦ Eve did not confess in her reply. The ancient Chinese held that the last four errors (wrongs), which Adam and Eve did not depart from evil and do good, were sins.[109]

Therefore, 罪 (sin, crime) was made with 四 (four, four times) and 非 (error, wrong).

9. 杏 (the tree of knowledge of good and evil)

A character was made to stand for the tree of knowledge of good and evil, thus its name was recorded.

Eating of the tree of knowledge of good and evil comprised three steps: ① they approached and stood beneath the tree; ② they took of it and ate; ③ after they ate, their eyes were opened.

The relative positions of 口 (mouth, eat) and 木 (fruit, tree) were changed so that three character, which exactly represent the three steps, were formed. See below:

Table 11-1 The Formation of Three Characters

The relative position of 口 and 木	Character formed
① 口 is beneath 木	杏
② 口 is inside 木	束
③ 口 is on 木	呆

The three formed characters 杏, 束, and 呆 correspond to the three steps of eating.

Table 11-2 Three Steps of Eating of the Tree of Knowledge of Good and Evil

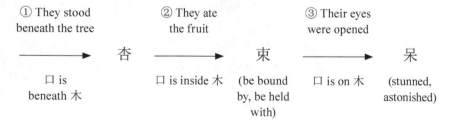

These three characters are just like three photographic films. When they are connected together, the whole process of Adam and Eve eating of the tree of knowledge of good and evil is showed like a film:

① 呆 means "be stunned, be astonished", and it corresponds to the third step and indicates their initial reaction. *The eyes of them both were opened, and they knew that they were naked*

(Gen. 3:7). At that moment, they must have been astonished and amazed to know that they were naked.

② 束 means "be bound by, be held with", it corresponds to the second step: they ate the fruit. Not to eat of the tree of knowledge of good and evil was the LORD's commandment. When they ate the fruit, they committed sin and were held by their sin. *His own iniquities shall ensnare the wicked, and he shall be holden with the cords of his sin* (Pro. 5:22).

③ 杏 corresponds to the first step: they turned close to and stood beneath the tree. In Chinese, 杏 means "apricot"[110]

ENDNOTES

1 See chapter 3, "Scripture Commentary 1: G-d Is Omniscient."
2 In the beginning, God created the dark void and threw divine sparks into it; and the sparks scattered and turned into all things—heaven and earth, the sea, and all that in them.
3 Abraham Cohen, *Everyman's Talmud*, trans. Gai Xun (Jinan: Shandong University Press, 2000), 43
4 Melvin Toka Yale, *The Jewish Singular Thought*, trans. Jiao Tingting (Beijing: China Social Science Press, 2009), 89.
5 Hans Christian Hu, *Das Bibelraetsel* (Shanghai: Xuelin Publishing House, 2006), 46.
6 Dee Dyas and Esther Hughes, *The Bible in Western Culture: The Student's Guide* (London and New York: Routledge, Taylor and Francis Group, 2005), 22.
7 See chapter 5, "Paradise Lost."
8 ① Concerning "offer the firstlings of the cattle to G-d": Exodus 13:2, 13; 34:19; Leviticus 27:26; Numbers 3:13; 8:17; Deuteronomy 12:6; 15:19. Concerning "offer the firstlings of the fruit of the ground to G-d": Exodus 23:19; 34:26; Leviticus 2:12, 14; 23:10, 17, 20; Numbers 15:20; 18:12; Deuteronomy 26:2, 10; ② See chapter 4, "Paradise Lost."
9 Psalm 63:1a
10 Isaiah 66:12
11 Ezekiel 3:12, 14
12 Psalm 139:8
13 Ezekiel 3:12, 14
14 Psalm 147:4
15 Isaiah 40:26
16 Job 38:33
17 Job 38:31–33
18 Job 38:16–17
19 Psalm 139:8
20 Job 38:8–11

21   Job 38:5–7

22   Job 38:19–20, 22

23   Job 38:24-27

24   Job 38:28-30

25   Psalm 139:1–18

26   Isaiah 41:19

27   Song of Songs 4:13–14

28   Isaiah 41:20

29   Exodus 20:2–8

30   Deuteronomy 24:20

31   Deuteronomy 24:21

32   Leviticus 19:10

33   Deuteronomy 23:14

34   Psalm 63:7–8

35   Psalm 131:2

36   Isaiah 55:12

37   Proverbs 8:30–31

38   See chapter 11, "From Eden to China'

39   ① See chapter 3, "Scripture Commentary 1: The First Prayer of Man"; ②
     see chapter 11, "Chinese Characters and Genesis: Pray For, Ask For."

40   Exodus 16:19b

41   The Talmud provides that the limit to the Sabbath's journey is within two
     thousand cubits from a person's house or domicile.

42   *Rosh Hashanah* and *Yom Kippur* are collectively called *Yamim Noraim.*

43   See chapter 11, "Chinese Characters and Genesis: It."

44   ① Exodus 32:19; ② Exodus 20:10b

45   The Talmud provides that the Sabbath ends at nightfall, approximately
     forty minutes after sunset.

46   These words pose an eternal question to every person. Where are you?
     Are you in your place on the Sabbath? Do you observe the mitzvah about
     journey limits on the Sabbath?

47   ① See chapter 6, "Sin and Punishment: The Departure and Return of
     Shechinah" and "Good and Evil"; ② see chapter 11, "Chinese Characters
     and Genesis: Sin, Crime."

48   Deuteronomy1:6–8

49   Isaiah 44:24

50   Isaiah 45:8

51   Isaiah 48:17–19

52   Isaiah 49:16

53   Isaiah 54:7–8

54   Deuteronomy 5:1, 6

55   Deuteronomy 5:7–15

56   Deuteronomy 5:17

57   Deuteronomy 6:1–2

58   Deuteronomy 11:10–12

59   Deuteronomy 11:18–21

60   Deuteronomy 15:19

61   Cain did not observe this statute. So the LORD did not look with favor on Cain and his offering.

62   Numbers 15:18–21

63   Deuteronomy 22:9–12

64   Deuteronomy 24:19–21

65   Deuteronomy 25:4

66   The ten generations after Adam did not observe the commandments well. The wickedness of man was great in the earth, and every imagination of the thoughts of his heart was only evil continually. So, G-d had to destroy the world by the Flood in 1656.

67   Deuteronomy 30:11–20

68   Hebrew word, the literal meaning of which is "dwelling." It refers to the appearance of G-d in the world. Abraham Cohen, trans. Gai Xun, *Everyman's Talmud* (Jinan: Shandong University Press, 2000), 44

69   See chapter 5, "Paradise Lost"; see chapter 11, "From Eden to China: Sin, Crime."

70   See chapter 7, "Scripture Commentary 2: The Self-Introduction of the LORD."

71   David Ruasvsky, *Modern Jewish Religious Movements*, trans. Fu Youde, Li Wei, Liu Ping (Jinan: Shandong University Press, 1996), 131

72   See chapter 5, "Paradise Lost"; see chapter 11, "Chinese Characters and Genesis: Sin, Crime."

73   Isaiah 41:20

74   Deuteronomy 11:2–4

75   See chapter 5, "Paradise Lost"

76 Li Zhichang, "The Modern Interpretation of the Bible—Viewed from 'the Curse of Canaan,' " *Biblical Literature Studies I*, (Beijing: People's Literature Publication House, 2007), p. 111.

77 Marvin Tokayer, *Hashkafah & Jewish Thought*, trans. Jiao Tingting (Beijing: China Social Science Press, 2009), 62.

78 See chapter 8, "The Legend of Noah."

79 Xu Xiangyun and Xu Meijuan, "Foundation of the Theory of Continental Drift and Its Significance in the Epistemology as Well as the Status in the History of Science," *Journal of Shenyang Institute of Engineering (Social Science) 3,* (Shenyang, Shenyang Institute of Engineering, 2007), 323–326.

80 See chapter 6, "Sin and Punishment: The Departure and Return of Shechinah."

81 Genesis 34:1. This verse implies that Dinah coveted the nations.

82 See chapter 6, "Sin and Punishment: The Departure and Return of Shechinah."

83 Fu Youde, *Modern Jewish Philosophy* (Beijing: People Publishing House, 1999), 135.

84 Genesis 15:5

85 Genesis 50:26

86 Exodus 32:12

87 Deuteronomy 3:26

88 Genesis 18:27

89 Genesis 18:25

90 Genesis 18:32

91 www.chabad.org/parshah/in-depth/default_cdo/aid/35860/jewish/In-Depth.htm

92 Micah 1:4

93 Genesis 1:2a

94 Song of Songs 2:13; 7:13–14

95 Psalm 104:30

96 Psalm 102:26

97 Robert Alter, *The Art of Biblical Narrative* (Beijing: The Commercial Press, 2010), 15.

98 N. Meifang, "On Chapter 38 of the Book of Genesis," *Foreign Literature 2* (Beijing, Beijing Foreign Studies University, 2011), 132–136.

[99]   http://baike.baidu.com/view/273081.htm

[100]   http://huaban.com/pins/3411599

[101]   Exodus 3:5; Joshua 5:15

[102]   W. Gunther Plant, *The Torah: A Modern Commentary* (New York: Union for Reform Judaism, 1981), 415–416.

[103]   J. H. Hertz, *The Pentateuch and Hafrorahs: Hebrew Text, English Translation and Commentary*, 2nd edition (London: Soncino, 1981), 221

[104]   Exodus 19:1–8

[105]   Exodus 19:16

[106]   Exodus 18:2

[107]   C. K. Kang and Ethel R. Nelson, *The Discovery of Genesis* (St. Louis: Concordia Publishing House, 1979), 25

[108]   See chapter 5, "Paradise Lost."

[109]   ① See chapter 5, "Paradise Lost"; ② see chapter 6, "Sin and Punishment: Good and Evil."

[110]   ① *Apricot* is *shaqed* (watcher) in Hebrew and originated from the verb *shaqad* (alert, awake, egersis). ② *Apricot* appears twice in the Torah: Exodus 25:32–34 and Numbers 17:1–8.

ABOUT THE AUTHOR

Yong Zhao, associate Professor at the School of Environmental Science and Engineering (Tianjin University, China), has a doctoral degree in chemical engineering from Tianjin University

Printed in the United States
By Bookmasters